MAXIMUM SECURITY

MAXIMUM SECURITY

Steven Linscott
with Randall L. Frame

CROSSWAY BOOKS • WHEATON, ILLINOIS
A DIVISION OF GOOD NEWS PUBLISHERS

Maximum Security.

Copyright © 1994 by Steven Linscott and Randall L. Frame.

Published by Crossway Books
          a division of Good News Publishers
          1300 Crescent Street
          Wheaton, Illinois 60187.

Cover photography: Robert M. Lightfoot III

Cover design: Russ Peterson

Art Direction: Mark Schramm

First printing, 1994

Printed in the United States of America

Unless otherwise indicated, Scripture quotations are taken from the HOLY BIBLE: NEW INTERNATIONAL VERSION®. Copyright © 1973, 1978, 1984 by International Bible Society. Used by permission of Zondervan Publishing House. All rights reserved.

The "NIV" and "New International Version" trademarks are registered in the United States Patent and Trademark Office by International Bible Society. Use of either trademark requires the permission of International Bible Society.

Library of Congress Cataloging-in-Publication Data
Linscott, Steven.
    Maximum security / Steven Linscott with Randall L. Frame.
       p.   cm.
    1. Linscott, Steven. 2. Prisoners—Illinois—Biography.
3. False arrest—Illinois—Case studies. 4. Murder—Illinois—Case studies. 5. Prisoners' families—Illinois—Case studies. 6. Trust in God. I. Frame, Randy. II. Title.
HV9468.L56A3 1994   364.1'523'092—dc20   93-41997
ISBN 0-89107-787-1

02		01		00		99		98		97		96		95		94
15	14	13	12	11	10	9	8	7	6	5	4	3	2	1

This book is dedicated to our family and friends, without whose love and support the outcome may have been different.

Our parents—
Paul and Teresa Linscott
and
Roy and Ruth Beverly

Ron and Joan Baines
Jim and Marge Chesney
Carl and Carol Craveiro
Tom Decker
Eleanor Findlay
E. L. Goss
Gordon and Nancy Haresign
Gary and Carol McLean
Richard McLeese
John and Evelyn Montgomery
Bob Ramey
Joe and Sharon Ritchie
Bob and Patti Sprinkle
Richard Widick

Good News Mission chaplains Russell Stroup,
Rick Gawenda, Chuck Haley, Steve Thompson

Cherry Hills Baptist Church, Springfield, Illinois
First Baptist Church, Centralia, Illinois
Laflin Gospel Chapel, Chicago
LaGrange Gospel Chapel, LaGrange, Illinois
Village Church (formerly River Forest Bible
Chapel), Oak Park, Illinois

And to all the many thousands of people around the
world who have supported us with their prayers.

CONTENTS

PREFACE

THIS BOOK IS WRITTEN in the first person because it is Steve's story. Randy's role was meticulously to follow the events described and to help Steve put them into words.

It would have been a challenge for us to make up a story with as many twists and turns, with as many high and low points, with as much drama, emotion, and suspense as the true story told in these pages.

It is a story that grapples with perhaps the most profound paradox associated with Christian living. For it is a testimony of firm belief in a God who controls even the most minute details of the universe. And yet there is a sense in which we must assert that in this universe a young woman should not have been killed and a young man should not have been falsely accused, convicted, and jailed.

With this paradox in mind, through this account of a most unusual journey of faith, we hope to affirm Christians' responsibility to change this world that God controls, beginning with ourselves. For those who have suffered for various reasons and who have struggled with unanswered questions about God, perhaps this story will prove helpful.

We owe a debt of gratitude to those whose books, articles, and thoughts lent shape and form to this story. Most of them are mentioned at various points in the book. We'd especially like to credit Gordon Haresign, whose book *Innocence* served as an extremely helpful reference to legal and other details regarding the early years of the case.

Thank you to Ted Griffin and Len Goss at Crossway Books for believing in and caring for the manuscript, and to Jeron Frame and Bob Ramey for their proofreading efforts.

We'd especially like to thank our children—Katherine, Paul, Vicki, Rachel, Annalyn, Rennie, and Marlise—who ran into many a closed door while one dad or the other was holed up behind a VDT. We pray, hope, and believe that all our sacrifices will be worthwhile as people discover through this story guidance, strength, courage, and inspiration for their own battles.

Randall D. Frame

Steven P. Linscott

INTRODUCTION

I N 1975, AS A NAVY SAILOR aboard the *U.S.S. Oklahoma City*, the flagship of the American Seventh Fleet, I spoke with a friend who had been through Navy SEAL training. The purpose of this training program is to teach a man to endure more than he'd ever imagined he could endure, and then some.

Those who supervise the SEALS-in-training accomplish their task by driving sailors to the absolute edge of physical endurance and mental sanity. When they reach that edge, the trainer pulls back, allowing for a time of rest and recovery. But not for long. Soon the sailors are dancing again on the border of madness and absolute physical exhaustion. They are driven, once more, as far as they can go, but never too far.

Recognizing the edge is a virtual art form. The trainer is the artist, molding young men, admonishing them first to reach for their ultimate limits and then to extend them. Each time the edge gets pushed farther and farther out. What was once challenging becomes routine. The difficult becomes easy. Growth never dreamed of becomes imaginable. The impossible starts to happen.

Among the SEALS, the saying goes, "If you can run five miles, you can run fifty." Many who have been through the program are living proof that the saying is true. But, as the training method suggests, if you try to go straight from five to fifty, you'll die.

I cannot count the number of times the illustration of the SEALS came to mind during the twelve years of my ordeal of false accusation—guilty verdict—imprisonment, an ordeal that continues to shape my life, my understanding of God and the world, and my faith.

Though I never volunteered for the program, I realized at several junctures during my years of crisis that I was in a sense a SEAL. And had I known from the beginning that it would fall to me to run the full fifty miles, I don't know how I could have survived. Maybe that is why so many urban street kids don't survive, why they give up on life so quickly. They are not blessed with the ignorance of not knowing what will happen next. They find it too easy to envision themselves behind bars, on drugs, or shot up in a gang war, because they've seen that reality in their families and their peers. Perhaps they know too much and thus become unwilling victims of cruel, self-fulfilling prophecy.

But that was not my reality. Having grown up in rural Maine, I never imagined spending time in a maximum security prison, where "success" was defined in terms of staying alive from day to day while managing to avoid becoming a victim of sexual assault. Nor could I envision being separated from my wife and my children during the crucial, formative years of marriage and family life.

Time and time again I was pushed to the limit of all I could take of fear, of confusion, of intense loneliness and hopelessness.

Unlike a SEAL, I did not have the option of quitting. For this was not an experiment. It was my life.

Yet, every time I reached the breaking point, something would happen that gave me the strength to carry on. Sometimes it was a letter from a friend or new insight into a passage of Scripture that I'd read a hundred times before, insight I cannot help but attribute to the intervention of God.

Or hope might come in the form of a positive legal development. We learned to live as hardened cynics amid the almost whimsical ups and downs of the legal system, which more than once tempted us to believe the end was just around the corner when in fact it was nowhere in sight. Sometimes—many times—hope would be dashed, but only after having served its purpose of getting me through a difficult day or an emotional state of mind.

As a SEAL inevitably develops an intense relationship with his trainer, so I was forced to develop my relationship with God. In times of true crisis, there is no other way. For me, the necessity of growing spiritually, or at least attempting to grow, was the only way I could begin to understand why all this was happening.

In this relationship, God, like a trainer of SEALS, was at once the source of my pain and my only hope for relief. My emotions toward Him ranged from fear, anger, and even hatred as we drew close to the edge, to profound love and deep trust as we pulled back.

Through it all I was very conscious of the fact that either my faith meant nothing or it meant everything. There was and is no in-between. And if it meant everything, then it was up to me to understand, as best I could, that a trainer of SEALS first has to make a man forsake what he is in order to begin rebuilding him into the person he wants to become. Underlying all of this was the confidence that I was not suffering alone, that God on the Cross had hurt and continued in some way to hurt for me far more than I could hurt for myself.

From a human point of view, I cannot help but wonder what my life would be like today had I never been drafted into a SEAL-type of ordeal. Perhaps I would be on the mission field. Or back in Maine, pastoring a church. Maybe I would be more "successful" than I have been up to now. Or maybe I would be sputtering along, going through the motions, spouting truisms, but beneath the surface questioning the validity and relevance of my faith.

Should I consider myself unfortunate to have suffered as I have? Or should I consider myself privileged to be singled out by God? Actually, I have learned the fruitlessness of trying to answer such questions. Rainer Maria Rilke wrote:

> Be patient toward all that is unsolved in your heart . . . try to love the questions themselves, like locked rooms and like books written in a very foreign tongue. Do not now seek answers, which cannot be given you because you would not be able to live them. And the point is to live everything. Live the questions now. Perhaps you will then gradually, without noticing it, live along some distant day into the answers.

True spiritual maturity does not mean having all the answers, but rather learning to live with questions. To me, answering the question, "Why me?" lost its luster long ago. Nor do I claim to have answers as a result of my experience that others do not or cannot have.

I do know that during my time of need, God used others, living and dead, to instruct and comfort me. I share my testimony in this book out of a desire to be a similar source of encouragement and inspiration to others. For in some sense, we are all

SEALS aboard the same boat in a stormy, stormy sea. And we owe one another all the guidance, all the love and help, we can offer.

1

A Murder and a Dream

The life of faith is not like opening Christmas presents every day. God's surprises disrupt; they humble; they amaze; they delight; and they come mixed up in messy ways with irritations and anguish.

Harold Myra

N UNEXPECTED KNOCK on the door ranks among life's minor mysteries. The brief moments between the knock and the answering carry with them a sort of low-grade suspense that inevitably accompanies the unknown.

In these moments active minds run rampant with possibilities. Is it a neighbor in search of a cup of sugar? An unexpected visit from a childhood friend? Most times it's something in between those extremes. It's more likely to be the neighbor than the long-lost friend. Indeed, the overwhelming majority of unexpected visits are eminently forgettable.

My wife, Lois, and I, along with our two young children (Katherine, two, and Paul, nine months), were going about business as usual one afternoon when we heard the doorbell to our apartment. The date was October 4, 1980. We had no reason to think anything was out of the ordinary. We had no way of knowing that this seemingly innocent, minor interruption would introduce an avalanche of turmoil into our lives.

I was at the typewriter when the doorbell rang, working on a term paper for one of my classes at Emmaus Bible College, which at the time was located in Oak Park, Illinois, near Chicago. Lois had been cleaning the kitchen. She arrived at the door as I was unlocking it.

There stood two uniformed police officers. Earlier we had noticed some police cars and fire engines parked in front of the building next to ours. Men in suits also hovered about the scene. One of the residents in our building had surmised they were FBI. We were soon to discover what all the fuss was about.

The officers informed us that not far away (in fact, it was two doors away) a woman had been murdered. They wanted to know if we had seen or heard anything unusual. "No, we've been busy here all day," Lois responded in her usual light but direct manner of speaking.

The officers corrected Lois's presumption that the crime had occurred during the day. "No, at about 1 this morning," one of them said. I told him we were all in bed by then.

We would learn later that the victim's neighbor had heard voices and stirrings next door in the wee hours of the morning. But apparently, except for the approximate time of the murder, the officers knew nothing.

They asked if others lived in our building, which was called the Austin Center. It was a sort of halfway house for men who had become Christians while in prison and were now trying to make the transition back into society. Lois and I, part of a staff of four, managed the property and served as houseparents in exchange for free rent. We assured the officers we would ask around and get back to them if we came up with something we thought would be helpful.

When the issue is murder, good investigators understandably want to uncover everything. Seemingly irrelevant clues—something somebody saw or heard or smelled—have been known to break cases. As they were leaving, the officers urged us to get back to them with anything that might prove useful, "no matter how silly it seems."

Were it not for that parting phrase, their visit would likely have joined the ranks of the insignificant. But as soon as I heard the words "no matter how silly it seems," a dream I'd had the night before jumped into my mind.

The dream was unusually intense and most unpleasant. It featured a light-complexioned man with short, blond hair, about five feet, six inches tall. He was wearing reddish brown pants and an off-white shirt that appeared to be made of terry cloth.

The room was softly lighted; it was a peaceful scene. The man seemed friendly at first. He was at ease as he talked with a second person in the dream, whose face remained blurred throughout and whose gender was unclear. Suddenly the man's demeanor changed, and the mood of the dream turned ominous.

From behind his back, the man produced some sort of object, and he smiled an evil smile as he held it in front of the other person's face. At that point I awoke. I checked the time; it was 2 A.M. I was disturbed by the dream, and tried for a few minutes to clear it from my mind, but as soon as I got back to sleep, the dream resumed, as intense as ever.

Now the man began assaulting his victim, beating the person repeatedly. The victim was surprised at first. But though the attack seemed unexpected, the victim offered little resistance. The brutal beating continued mercilessly as the victim fell to the floor. The dream left me with the final impression of blood flying everywhere.

I awoke once again. Thinking I'd heard a noise in the front room of our apartment, I went to check things out. I returned to bed and went back to sleep. This time the dream did not resume. However, the torrential chain of events it would launch was about to begin.

The following day, Sunday, I discussed the dream and the visit from the police with one of the counselors at the Austin Center. He urged me to consider the possibility that my dream was not a mere coincidence. He said it could have psychic significance. Noting that such dreams had proved helpful in solving crimes, he advised me at least to let the police know about it.

I considered his advice, but not seriously enough to act upon it. The next day, however, Lois and I went for a walk. Lois had read a newspaper article from the *Chicago Tribune* on the murder, and she gave me some of the details.

I had thought it unusual that I dreamed of a murder the same night a woman was being murdered nearby, perhaps even during the exact time of the killing. The newspaper account revealed additional similarities. The woman, Karen Ann Phillips, twenty-four years of age, had been beaten to death—as in the dream—with a blunt instrument. In addition, according to the *Tribune* report, police suspected that she knew her assailant. (Apparently there were no signs of forced entry.) This was consistent with the dream.

With this new information, I began leaning toward telling the police about the dream. I told Lois about my intentions. "I don't see anything wrong with that," she replied, noting that the police had asked for anything, "no matter how silly."

Over the years I would wonder many times if Lois truly felt

it was a good idea, or if she was hesitant to express her opinion. For back then, humility was not among my greatest attributes. As the leader of our household, I was less of a servant and more of a boss, I'm sure, than I ought to have been.

I talked the matter over with Carlos Craveiro, a friend who was also on staff at the Austin Center. Carlos did not take the whole matter very seriously at all. He suggested I might get a kick out of telling the police about the dream, and that they might get a good laugh out of it.

My hesitancy had nothing to do with fearing I would be accused of the crime. I had never been in trouble with the law, had received an honorable discharge from the Navy, and had positive relationships with virtually everyone I knew. At the time I had absolutely no concept that anyone could possibly think I was capable of killing another human being, let alone of beating to death someone I didn't know for no reason.

Rather, I was mainly concerned about making a fool of myself, about appearing to be playing stupid games when in fact a woman was dead and the killer was still at large.

On the other hand, I considered the unusual intensity of the dream. Perhaps it was from God. Perhaps it was a result of some extrasensory perception I was unaware I had. Perhaps God wanted to use me in some way to accomplish His purposes of justice, and thereby to witness to police and to the community. If that was the case, I thought, I had a responsibility to go forward. I figured the worst that could happen was that the police would tell me politely to please quit wasting their time. That, at least, would end my confusion about what to do.

After thinking a bit more about what everyone had said, I decided to call the police. It was about 9:30 on Monday evening, two days after the crime, when I picked up the phone. I had been pouring out words on a term paper and was ready for a break. As

I recounted the dream, the officer laughed. Not wanting to take myself too seriously, I laughed along with him.

Nevertheless, they were interested. They asked me to make a written account of the dream and they said someone would come by later that evening to pick it up. What was going on in their minds at that time I do not know. Perhaps even at that early stage, they were giving me rope with which to hang myself. I sat down and composed the following account:

> I had a dream Saturday evening [actually Friday] in which I saw a man bludgeon a person to death.
>
> The man was blond-haired, fair features, the hair was short; the man is square-built, not muscular but good size. About 5' 5" to 5' 7" wearing a terry cloth, short-sleeve shirt with two or three narrow horizontal lines across the chest. His pants were brown (dark) or reddish-brown. The man was easy-going in character and was at ease with the person.
>
> The person struck seems to me to have been struck while lying down or crouching and to have been hit on the head (the side) (possibly on the right hand, though I'm not sure).
>
> The person struck seems not to have given a lot of resistance. She has an air of acceptance or peace. She clearly wasn't expecting the attack. I note this from the change in the person attacking, as he was calm and at ease with the victim before the attack, and quick and brutal during the attack. The person was struck a number of times. The last impression I have of the attack was the bludgeon striking bleeding flesh and a lot of blood flying. The person struck seems to be black, though I'm not sure.
>
> Secondary impressions are of the attacker in the first stages, the quieting stage, the easygoing stage, as having a light on behind him and to the left as I see him, and lower than his head. It makes a soft glow in the room. I can't get any impressions on the rest of the room except that it seems to be a living room; a couch seems to be present to the left of the light.

As I dreamt, the first stage was very clear, but I woke up as I sensed a change come over the person, and I tried to shake off the dream and go back to sleep. I went to sleep again and dreamt of the attack. After this I awoke and was very disturbed because of the vividness of the dream. I thought I heard a noise in our front room of our apartment and so I got up and went out and came back and went to sleep.

Concerning the second stage of the dream, the attacker is striking down the victim. She is below his waist and then below the knees and does not give much resistance to this attack.

When the officers came by to pick up my account of the dream, they were all business. They were courteous enough but offered no smiles. They said they were not sure if or how they would be able to make use of what I had just given them. They wanted to discuss it with some experts. They asked if I would be able to stop by the station sometime to discuss the dream further.

I told them I was busy but was willing to help in any way I could. They said they would work around my schedule. "This is fascinating," I remarked as they were about to leave. They agreed. We shook hands. They were on their way. And, unknowingly, I had entered the fray.

The next day one of the officers called. "We've been in touch with a psychic," he said, adding that he thought the dream could be relevant. He said they wanted to get a clearer description of the killer from the dream, and they wanted any further impression I could provide. "It's always possible that when we question you, things will come to mind that you weren't aware of," I remember one of the officers telling me.

I would learn later that in all likelihood I was a suspect— rather, *the* suspect—right from the beginning. But at the time I had no fears or suspicions of the officers' motives. Instead, I viewed this opportunity to help police in the same way I viewed any opportunity to interact with others—as a chance perhaps to lead an officer or two to Christ.

I scheduled an appointment at the police station for 4 P.M. the following day. My association with the criminal justice system had begun innocently enough. But in the coming months and years, that innocence would be stripped away amid unimaginable confusion and turmoil.

Our plans to go to the mission field would melt away in the heat of my battle for freedom and, at times, for my very survival. My life—and the lives of my wife and children—would be changed forever. Like Navy SEALS, we would be taken to the very limits of our strength.

2

The Inquisition

It is better we should not know our future. If we did, we
should often spoil God's plan for our life. . . . It is better to
walk, not knowing, with God, than it would be to see the
ways and choose for ourselves.

J. R. Miller

ABOUT SIX THOUSAND years ago a man named Joseph
had a few unusual dreams. He dreamt of eleven sheaves
of corn—one for each of his brothers—bowing down to
his. He dreamt of the sun, moon, and eleven stars—again, his
brothers—genuflecting in his direction. His brothers so appreciated Joseph's disclosure of his dreams that they sold him into
slavery. Had Joseph kept his dreams to himself, he would have
been spared a lot of agony. And perhaps also a lot of fulfillment
and joy.

As my life progressed, I would develop a closer and closer
relationship with this kindred spirit, this patriarch who lived in
another place and another time but whose life experiences in
some ways paralleled my own.

From all we can tell, Joseph was a man of God, well-
equipped with both earthly wisdom and a deep sense of spirituality. But like any good protagonist, he had a tragic flaw. Kinder

Biblical scholars label it "self-assurance" or "overconfidence." Some have called it "arrogance."

In some ways I could identify with Joseph's character flaw. I have no recollections of ever struggling with a poor self-image as a child, teenager, or young man. I succeeded in Little League, in school, and at enough other endeavors that I never hesitated to try something new.

When I became a Christian on November 24, 1974 at the age of twenty, this self-assurance carried over. I quickly mastered the basic teachings of the Bible. People regularly came to the Lord as a result of my witnessing efforts. I enjoyed success as a Bible study leader and as a leader in general. People came to me for advice. I had this Christianity thing down pretty well.

Later, reflecting on those times from a prison cell, I would have a different idea about how successful I was. I would come to appreciate a distinction between being religious and understanding God, between succeeding at ministry and truly grappling with God's purposes for my life. I would come to realize that I, like Joseph, possessed a streak of arrogance.

I kept my appointment with destiny, arriving at the Oak Park police station at 4 P.M. on Wednesday, October 8. Not long after I got inside I walked past a man who was having his rights read to him, even though he did not appear to be under arrest. The man's house had just been burglarized, one of the officers explained, and he'd come in to make a statement. The officer, Detective Robert Scianna, added that anyone making a statement is routinely read his rights. He proved his point by reading me my rights. To this day, I do not know if this is routine policy or if this was part of the setup.

We started the evening off with some Cokes and small talk. The officers—Scianna and Detective Ronald Grego—politely thanked me for coming in, then began asking about the dream.

The kinds of questions they asked required that I go well beyond the boundaries of the dream. They wanted me to give them my impressions of the assailant. They wanted to know about his personality, his temperament, his state of mind. "Get inside his head," they said.

Then they asked the same kinds of questions about the victim in my dream. Was she religious? Where did she grow up? What were her interests? Except for any impressions I recalled from the dream, my answers by necessity consisted totally of speculation. I wondered how my conjecture could possibly be helpful, but the officers assured me that this kind of brainstorming session was standard procedure when questioning psychics.

My acceptance of their working hypothesis that I was psychic, I am convinced, contributed to their perception of greater similarity between my dream and the crime than actually existed. In my written account of the dream, for example, I began by using the word "person" in reference to the victim, because the victim's gender was not revealed in the dream. But after learning that the victim was a woman, it was hard not to use "she" and "her" in discussing the crime. Again, this was a concession to the working hypothesis.

The same kind of thing happened with my use of the word "bludgeon." At the time, that word was not in my vocabulary, but it was the word used in the *Chicago Tribune* article to describe the murder. I don't know how much of my late-night speculation at the police station was actually based on things I'd learned about the crime in the few days since it had happened. But I know it must have contributed to the false perception of similarity.

That first night their questions and my "answers" went on for three hours. At one point they asked if in my dream I was actually there, if I was splashed with the victim's blood, but before I could consider a reply they moved on to something else. When I got home and told Lois about what had happened, she raised a red flag. "Do the police regard you as a suspect?" she asked. I laughed it off.

The next day, however, while I was sitting in class it struck me for the first time that Lois's concern was legitimate. The line of questioning, I realized, was consistent with the possibility that they thought I was their man.

I decided to speak with Russell Stroup, a prison chaplain and the Chicago area director of the Good News Mission, a prison ministry. He advised me to proceed with some caution, but said he thought I had nothing to worry about.

Nevertheless, when Officer Scianna called me that afternoon, I immediately asked if they regarded me as a suspect. His response was just as immediate: "No." I felt better. I would learn later, however, that even at this early stage the investigations to pursue other possible suspects had stopped. None of the victim's acquaintances or neighbors were seriously considered, nor were any of the ex-convicts at the Austin Center. A known rapist who lived in the vicinity of the victim's apartment and who was undergoing psychiatric treatment was never questioned, even though the police knew about him.

Years later we found out that a close friend of Karen's, Faye Codding, had called police with information pertaining to the murder investigation. Faye had roomed with Karen in college, and she reported that Karen had been raped as a college student. Because of this, according to Faye, Karen was extremely careful. Faye told police she was convinced Karen would never have allowed someone to enter her apartment, especially after midnight, unless she knew the person very well. (This was significant given that there were no signs of forced entry.)

But Faye's call to the police was made on October 16, twelve days after the murder and well after they latched on to me. And thus it was totally ignored.

Some Oak Park journalists speculated years later that the police had a vested interest in arresting a white person for the crime, given the political and social tensions associated with integration in that section of Oak Park in 1980. Whatever the reasons, the case was closed soon after I set foot in the police station. And the only one there who didn't know it was me.

"No," Scianna had responded to my point-blank query. And then he asked me to come in again, partly because they wanted me to help with a composite sketch of the supposed killer. This, I felt, was a reasonable request. Again, given their stated belief that I was a psychic, it made sense that they could benefit from a description of the possible killer. Though I was a bit more skeptical, I still wanted to help. Besides, to reject their request would imply I had something to hide.

After telling Lois that I'd be back shortly, I returned to the police station at about 6 P.M.

For the first hour and a half I labored to describe the assailant from my dream to a police artist. It was a process that probably should have taken only fifteen minutes. But the artist regularly asked for clarifications of my words of description. Looking back on it, I realize the man was trying to manipulate my statements wherever he could in order to draw the sketch *he* wanted to draw. He looked at me often as he worked, and when his masterpiece was completed—surprise, surprise!—it bore some resemblance to the man on whose words it was supposedly based—*me*. He would later add sideburns and glasses to make the resemblance even closer.

I began to get very suspicious and was, in fact, ready to leave. But they asked me to go over the dream one more time. "Just once more, quickly," I replied, becoming agitated. This time when they read me my rights I felt a bit more threatened. But again, I thought that to refuse to cooperate now would make them suspect me for sure. "No, I do not wish to consult a lawyer or to have anyone present," I said firmly. "I have absolutely nothing to hide."

Officer Scianna, perhaps sensing my frustration, tried to put me at ease. He said it was "remarkable" how much help I was providing them. "The last time you had some pretty strong impressions that helped us in our investigation of this crime," he said, "and I was hoping maybe we could go through this again, if you don't mind."

I began going over some of the same ground covered during the first session. This time an assistant state's attorney, Jim McCarter, was present, but that did not strike me as unusual. Though I was more guarded against the possibility that they considered me a suspect, I still believed I was helping them solve the crime. Perhaps I believed it because that is what I wanted to believe.

As their questions got more and more detailed, I became less and less willing to grasp at straws, to answer just for the sake of answering. The tapes of the conversations bear this out, as time after time my replies consisted of such disclaimers as "I don't know" and "I'm not sure."

I could not understand how this was helping them find someone else. Their persistence led me, more and more, to suspect that the one they were trying to "find" was me. Finally I spoke my mind, expressing my concern about their line of questioning by again asking, "Do you suspect me of this crime?"

This time the reply did not come right away. After an uncomfortable pause, all three started talking at the same time. The detectives yielded the floor to the state's attorney.

His response was fairly long-winded. "We don't suspect you," McCarter said, adding that I was "the key to this case" and that the information I had already provided to the investigators was "invaluable at this point." He also said that in the event I was ever to appear as a witness in court, I had to be eliminated as a suspect. I took this as an explanation for their suspicious questions.

He reminded me that no one had yet been arrested for the murder. He said that the investigators talking with me "may be able to jog something in your memory that can give them a clue. That's what we are attempting to do at this point."

The officers pitched in, doing their part to quell my concern. Again they referred to my possible psychic ability. At one point when I tried to turn the discussion to my Christian faith, Scianna played along, suggesting that God was at work in the interview.

Though their efforts kept me going, they did not erase my concerns. I wanted it to end; I wanted to walk out. In retrospect, I realize I was in an impossible situation. I was outnumbered three to one and, at twenty-four, was younger than any of the three. Plus, they were in positions of authority, positions that all my life I'd been trained to respect.

But that respect had limits. When they asked whether the killer might have a split personality, I again interjected. "To be honest with you, I kind of wonder at your motives sometimes," I said, adding once more that I felt that their line of questioning seemed to be an attempt to implicate me.

Grego responded by assuring me that things were not what they seemed. If they were asking questions that implied I was a suspect, he said, they were doing it unknowingly. "If we had a lead on you, you know, these officers would not be sitting here without handcuffs," McCarter chimed in, "and you wouldn't be walking out of here shortly."

But then he proceeded to ask if I would be willing to let them take a sample of my blood, saliva, and hair. They also wanted to look in my car. I was growing ever more certain that despite their assurances to the contrary, they considered me a suspect. On the other hand, they had said that if I was to be credible in court, they would have to eliminate me as a suspect.

Whatever they were thinking, at that point the bottom line for me was that I had nothing to hide. If it took blood and hair samples to end their suspicions, I was up for that. I agreed to do it, but I asked to call Lois first. It was 11:30, and she hadn't heard from me all evening. When at first they wouldn't let me call my wife, I refused to cooperate any further until they did.

Upon answering the phone, Lois had an urgent message for me: "Get out of there right away." It seems she had had some visitors during the evening: senior state's attorney Jay Magnuson and two plainclothes officers. They told Lois they were in consultation with a psychiatric professional in California and wanted to know more about my dreams. They looked around the Austin Center, including our apartment. They asked Lois about my religious experiences and whether I'd ever done drugs. At first Lois trusted them, but then, as I did, she began to grow suspicious, especially when they asked if I had any terry cloth shirts. Lois showed them the only shirt I had with any terry cloth in it at all. They looked at it briefly but showed no further interest in it.

After they finally left, Lois had repeatedly called the police station, but no one would patch her through to me. Each time they said I wouldn't be long. At about 10:30 she'd called Chaplain Stroup to tell him what was happening. He advised Lois to tell me at her first opportunity to leave the station.

I tried to heed that advice. But as I got up to go, Officer Scianna grabbed my keys and wallet. He pushed me face first against the wall, pulling my arm up behind my back. "You're not going anywhere," he said. All night long I'd been in over my head. Now I finally realized it.

I demanded to speak with a lawyer but settled for Chaplain Stroup. He arrived bleary-eyed sometime between 12:30 and 1:00 A.M. I didn't see him right away. They took him to another room and showed him pictures of Karen Phillips. They urged him to advise me to provide the blood, hair, and saliva samples they'd asked for. Chaplain Stroup obliged. Agreeing with me that I had nothing to hide, he suggested I cooperate and end this thing.

So off we went, along with officers Grego and Scianna, to a local hospital. After they got what they wanted, we returned to the police station. By now it was nearly 3 A.M. But the night was yet young.

They asked Chaplain Stroup to remain in the reception area, and before I knew it I was back in the interview room after being fingerprinted. Finally the masquerade was over. Officer Grego opened up: "Steve, I'm going to say my piece, okay? You've cooperated with us as much as you can, as much as you say you know, okay? I'd like to think that you are a person who knows he needs help, okay? My partner and I and everyone else is convinced that you killed this young lady, okay?"

"You're kidding," was my first response. He was not.

"The evidence you gave us tonight will convict you," he said, adding, "If we have to come back and get you with an arrest warrant, the judge will see that you did not request any help."

I began shouting, "Analyze the evidence! Analyze your evidence first!"

They assured me that analysis of the physical evidence

would reveal I was the murderer. Tired, angry, and now getting scared, I requested on tape that Chaplain Stroup be present. Request denied. "You sit here," screamed Grego. "We're not asking you anything . . . Now just sit there and shut up. Nobody's asking you questions. You're going to be arrested for this."

Then it was Scianna's turn. He said he was going to go over the evidence with me. As I tried to speak, he shouted, "I don't want you to say anything. When you want to say something, you tell us and we'll get a counselor for you. I don't want to hear nothing from you. Don't say anything. Just look."

I refused to look as he showed grisly pictures of the murdered woman and the crime scene. He drew comparisons between details revealed or implied by the pictures and my testimony. Holding up the sketch drawn by the police artist he asked sarcastically, "Does this look like anybody in this room?"

Immediately I reminded Scianna that earlier I'd disclaimed any resemblance between the artist's sketch and the image from my dream. Next he claimed that on the first night of questioning I'd worn a shirt like the one I'd described the dream killer as wearing. I considered this claim ridiculous. The shirt from the dream was all terry cloth and had two or three horizontal lines across the chest. The one I'd worn had terry cloth only on the sleeves and had no stripes across the chest.

But by then I'd realized arguing with them was useless. Against my will, the officers proceeded down their list of reasons for concluding that I was the killer. This fiasco had begun more than eight hours ago, and I was emotionally exhausted. Nothing I might say could make a difference; they had already made up their minds. But when I tried to leave, they again blocked my path.

It sometimes happens that a psychologically troubled killer unable to deal with his guilt will approach authorities, as I had done, somehow disguising his role in the crime but ultimately looking for the right opportunity to confess. Perhaps they truly believed I was the killer and were genuinely confused that I had not confessed by now. More threatening to me was the possibility that they did not particularly care about the truth. Perhaps they believed they could make the charges stick whether or not I was the right person. For all I knew, perhaps they were not above doctoring the physical evidence to make it fit their theories. They had certainly done that with my testimony concerning the dream.

I would learn later (at my trial) that at about the same time I was at the hospital giving hair and blood samples, other investigators were at the scene of the crime removing the bloodstained section of the carpet. For almost four days that carpet was locked up at the Oak Park police station in the same room with the envelope containing my hair. That envelope had not been sealed in my presence.

Grego continued his assault: "If you never called us, we would not have known where to go. You came to us. You want help." Then he waxed theological. "You want God to give you penance," he said. "You want Him to redeem you."

After I told him again that I had no feelings of guilt surrounding murder, he threatened, "You are going to get the electric chair. The judge is going to see that you have no remorse in your soul. It's very embarrassing, too, what you did. It's a vicious crime, but it's embarrassing. Your wife will become embarrassed, your chaplain will become embarrassed. It's very embarrassing, very embarrassing."

As much as I should have remained quiet, my instincts were to challenge his statements. He had an answer for everything. I asked what possible motive I could have for committing this crime. Apparently drafting a theory to fit his conclusions, Grego responded, "You went over there, you got in the apartment, you spoke with her, you talked about sex. You found out there was going to be no sex—willingly—so you beat her to death, and you beat her and struck her. That's why she was killed. That's why she was killed, because she would not give you any sex."

Finally, after I stated once again for the record that I did not kill anyone, Grego announced that the interview was over. Lois, who'd persisted in calling the station, finally got word at about 4:30 A.M. that they were letting me go. That word came from state's attorney Magnuson, who informed her that he was sending me home even though I was a "very dangerous person" with "three personalities." We later wondered if he would have sent me home if he truly believed that.

When I got home, I told Lois about what to that point was the most terrible night of my life. There would be many others. I knew that the truth was on my side, but truth sometimes feels like a weak companion. Six thousand years ago the truth was on Joseph's side too. He'd been accused by Potiphar's wife of making sexual advances. She had one of his garments to "prove" it. The authorities didn't care to hear the story of how she came to possess that garment. She was politically well-positioned. That was all that mattered.

Yet Joseph understood something it would take me years to internalize. He understood that what matters most is that God knows the truth. And so each time his life took a turn for the worse, he did not despair or ask why. He accepted his lot, remained faithful, and tried to make the best of his circumstances.

This world is riddled with misunderstanding—among nations, among friends, between husbands and wives. Each of us has at one time or another been misunderstood or misperceived. Each of us has experienced the hurt that comes from being accused, like Joseph, of doing something wrong when in fact we were trying to do something right. How comforting it is to realize that when no one else understands or believes you, God does.

Faith like Joseph's enables us to take risks. Although his interpretation of his dreams got him into trouble, Joseph kept on dreaming and interpreting. And God used those dreams to make him the most powerful person in Egypt. Joseph did not allow a bad experience to prevent him from staying true to the path God had laid out for him.

Faith like Joseph's enables us to affirm that the powers of darkness and deceit may overcome temporarily, maybe even permanently in this life. But they cannot and will not prevail forever. I did not die in the electric chair as Grego had prophesied. And a few years after he made that prediction, amid allegations of scandal in the Oak Park Police Department, Officer Grego became the centerpiece of an investigation of corruption. He was dismissed without pay a year before he would have qualified to receive a pension.

3

In the Catacombs

Sometimes God calms the storm—and sometimes He lets
the storm rage and calms His child.

Anonymous

I CAN STILL HEAR the grinding gears of the police bus as it
pulled out of the underground vault area beneath the
courtroom and into the daylight. Even the smell of that
ride registered its own, lasting impression.

Not long before, I had read an account of a man who'd been
arrested. He described the "smell of fear," a pungent odor of
chemicals mixed with sweat. Now I could add my own personal
testimony in support of the argument that fear indeed has a
smell.

As the bus moved along, I felt numb, almost paralyzed. I
could hear my heart pounding through my shirt. Even though
the dark windows and iron grating prevented much of a view, I
could see parts of Oak Park flash by. After a short time on the
Interstate, the bus pulled off into an unfamiliar section of town,
weaving its way among decaying urban buildings riddled with
graffiti.

Yesterday I was a Bible school student, a missionary correspondent, a leader on campus, a devoted husband and father. Today, after being held by police and arrested for murder, I was in handcuffs and on my way to one of the world's largest and most dangerous prisons: Cook County Jail.

The arrest had come six weeks after the interrogation. I had felt obligated to let my parents know what was happening, so I called them from the police station. It was one of the toughest calls I've ever made. My mother, who is a very emotional person, had had some reservations about us moving off to the big city in the first place. This certainly didn't ease her concerns. She took the news hard.

Dad's a more practical person. I came away from talking with him feeling confident. Though he too took the news hard, he immediately began to discuss plans to deal with the problem. This gave me some assurance that the chaos I was experiencing would be brought under control.

Yesterday I had the world under my control. Things had not always gone right for me or for those with whom I came into contact. But no matter what came my way, I was prepared. I had a Scripture verse for virtually every situation, a ready response to any question or problem. After all, I was a leader, and that's what leaders were supposed to do.

But today the world was out of my control. I had no pat answers; in fact I had no answers at all. I felt totally inadequate to find comfort for myself, let alone to help others. As the bus rolled past the heavy, steel-wire gates and up to a set of dark brown doors, the cold realization came over me that short of God's intervention, I could die in this place.

Finally it was time for me and the others to disembark. We were led *en masse* down a steep incline that went underground. We moved along slowly, stopping frequently as other groups of marching prisoners, some of them no doubt "veterans," crossed our path. Eventually we arrived at some large holding cells, along with hundreds more who had come from jails or other points of departure throughout Chicago and environs.

At the direction of guards shouting instructions, we shed our civilian clothes and stood in line while they checked our body cavities for contraband. Then we were given generic, brown prison jumpers and ordered back into the holding cells. I tried, unsuccessfully, not to let my fear show through. One of the processors told me to tighten up my emotions and not look so scared. Strange advice to offer a leader.

Even those who have never been to prison have some idea of what it must be like. That concept serves as a deterrent. It would be an even greater deterrent if everyone could actually experience life in a maximum security institution, even for a day. The dining ambience leaves a lot to be desired. The food is every bit as good as you might expect, but the company is generally not the kind you hope will drop in on your family reunion.

Actually, some inmates are essentially good people who got caught up in circumstances they could not control. They lacked both a network of support and the strength to make it on their own.

Others are virtual evil incarnate, the kind who could have found their way to prison from any position of privileged status. It is almost as if this is their home, the place they want to be— perhaps for some, the place they feel they deserve to be.

Of course, those who are innocent belong to neither category. But in prison there is no such thing as an innocent man. The guards have learned instinctively to ignore stories of innocence.

Most of the drawbacks of prison life are fairly obvious. After years of deciding where to go on vacation, when to take a nap or go out for ice cream, such choices are suddenly stripped away. In prison, my children—my flesh and blood—became mere memories, as if from another life. Instead of having my wife as a roommate, I had thieves and gang members.

In prison, the pursuit of staying alive and remaining in one piece takes on a greater urgency. It requires more of a conscious effort. New prisoners who don't already know it learn quickly that no one can be trusted.

For Lois and me, however, the greatest challenges were emotional. Our world had shattered, had crumbled around us. It was as if we'd been living in a place like Eden, with the sun always shining and a cool wind blowing. Suddenly the world turned dark and threatening; the wind began to howl, giving rise to voices from within, evil voices that whispered, "God has abandoned you. You deserve this."

Upon entering prison, I'd convinced myself that before long this misunderstanding would be cleared up and I would be free. A week later I had a court date. It was a break from the daily routine, but hardly a refreshing one: awakened before dawn, thin grits for breakfast, then handcuffs and chains. Next came the forced march to the waiting area: more steel and glass. Chains on the feet did nothing to prevent fights from breaking out among the hundreds of prisoners bunched together.

The bus was a rolling cage, a jail on wheels. When we arrived at our destination, I waited in a lockup area at the rear of the courtroom until I heard my name called. My day in court lasted perhaps ten minutes, which went by in a blur. I returned to the jail, exhausted from the trip. That night I called Lois, and she carefully explained to my unwilling ears exactly what the term "No Bond" meant: I would not be released. Not today, not next week, perhaps not ever.

As this reality began to sink in, it was accompanied by the

most intense emotional pain I'd ever experienced. I was drained of all energy; I felt as if I were bleeding inside.

Despite the external hardships and challenges presented by prison life, the most dangerous confinement is that which emerges from within. After that first, disappointing court date, self-doubt began to wind its web around me. I was nagged by the thought that as a Christian committed to the truth, I had never considered the possibility that the police were right.

I knew I had no recollection of the crime. But what if I was "crazy"? What if I did not really know myself? What if I was, against my conscious will, suppressing from consciousness a reality I could not face?

I began to consider any and all facts that would support this theory, probing my very soul for clues that might point to my guilt. The police had arrested me only after analyzing the evidence. Though I did not know exactly what the supposed evidence revealed, this at least seemed to be a strike against me. I'd said that the killer from my dream wore a terry cloth shirt. I did not own a terry cloth shirt. But the one shirt I had with a bit of terry cloth on the sleeves I'd worn to the police station. Could that have been more than coincidence?

Lois and I had experienced the usual share of marital squabbles. Sometimes I held things in instead of communicating them. Was it possible that I'd repressed emotions for too long, and then had unloaded with a vengeance on someone I did not even know?

On the other hand, even if I could successfully hide this crime from myself, was it possible for me to hide it from Lois, too? Could I have gone out for milk—let alone to commit a murder—without her noticing? And as gruesome as the crime scene was, could I have pulled this off without getting even a drop of blood on my clothes or shoes, without leaving a single indisputable trace of physical evidence? Lois pretty much had my wardrobe memorized. She knew that nothing had been discarded.

As for my terry cloth shirt, it did not come close to fitting the description of the shirt I'd described from my dream. Besides, I wore that shirt often; there was nothing the least bit unusual about having worn it to the police station.

Nevertheless, I was confused, uncertain. Either I was innocent or I ranked right up there with the most skillful deranged killers ever to walk the earth.

Looking back, I find it easy to understand and put into perspective my emotional and psychological processes during that time. For one thing, prison itself is an unsettling, disorienting influence. As former hostages or Vietnam vets can testify, the emotional effects of trauma can be both unimaginable and unpredictable.

More significantly, that first experience behind bars presented me with a major case of cognitive dissonance. Psychologists know that the urge to resolve dissonance, to eliminate ambiguity, is a powerful urge. People are instinctively compelled to adjust their thinking and beliefs, even their behavior, in order to conform to the beliefs and thinking of others they hold in esteem.

For me, the dissonance centered in part around my high respect for authority. As a Christian, I believed that respect for governing and legal authorities was Biblical. And in all my dealings with the powers that be, I had never had any occasion to think that respect was ill-placed.

Not long after we'd moved to Chicago, for example, our apartment was burglarized. We lost all our Christmas gifts and the diamond ring I'd given to Lois upon our engagement. When the police officer who came over saw how distraught we were, he literally screamed into his police radio for a forensic expert to investigate. It confirmed my view that these people were my friends, that they were on my side.

My cognitive dissonance spanned the theological realm. I had great difficulty believing that God would allow something like this to happen to someone who, though far from perfect, was trying to serve Him. And if it is beyond God's nature to allow this, I reasoned, the only alternative was that I was guilty.

And so I searched myself—my thoughts, my actions, and my deepest feelings. At times the slightest hint of anything unusual or imperfect would offer itself up to resolve the dissonance. Up to this point in my ordeal, I believed that the truth was my friend. But now, in some strange way, it was my enemy: it prevented me from resolving this dissonance. In a way I envied those who were in prison because they had committed some atrocious crime. At least their imprisonment made sense to them. A legitimate, well-deserved prison term would be a relief compared to the pain and stress of my confusion.

At times I had the most haunting urges to confess. If I could only remember something to which I could confess, the dissonance would be resolved. One night, on the eve of a court date, I actually decided that when I got to court I would admit to having committed the crime. Moments later I recovered with a shock. I remember screaming at the bricks, the concrete, and bars, "Confess to what? There is nothing to confess!"

I was discovering that truth is not always convenient. It is not always a friend—it doesn't always bring pleasant circumstances our way. For me, to cling to the truth during this time entailed a great risk. It meant I would have to reevaluate my relationship with God, to deal with feelings of betrayal, to question His character. I would have to ask what Philip Yancey asked in his book *Disappointment with God*: "Is God unfair? Is God silent? Is God hidden?" The truth demanded that I approach this abyss, and it left me with no choice but to jump in.

Gradually I began to resolve my cognitive dissonance in other directions. Affirming along with Lois that God is holy and just, I opened my mind to the possibility that He still cared for me, that He had some greater purpose behind what He was asking me to endure. Affirming my innocence, I began to mistrust the authorities and to believe that something evil must be at work here. I developed feelings of hatred toward the police as I came to believe they had little regard for the truth.

Looking back on this time, I realize how misguided my spiritual life was at points.

During that time I was preoccupied, weighed down by my emphasis on my status as a sinner—saved by grace, but a sinner nonetheless. My prayer life was dominated by extended confessions of sin, almost to the point of excluding everything else. This was true to some extent even before my troubles with the law.

The day would arrive when I would understand and appreciate my primary identity as a citizen of Heaven. It was one of many priceless lessons yet to come.

4

Table Manners

When a man goes through a crisis he fears he is losing God, but instead of that he is beginning to see Him for the first time, and he sees Him as a grander, more marvelous being than ever he imagined.

Oswald Chambers

AMONG THE MOST underrated parts of the human body, in my estimation, are the hands. Except for concert pianists and artists, most of us take our hands for granted. With hands we touch and feel. Infants learn quickly how to use their hands for sustenance. We reach out and give with hands. And we cling to what we cannot—or will not—let go of.

Thomas à Kempis, in *The Imitation of Christ*, chose the metaphor of a "grasping hand" that clings to the things of this world. Our inability to let go prevents us from offering ourselves unfettered to Christ. That we should and must let go is easy to assert. It is much harder to do.

Even in prison there are things to hang on to. For example, as prisoners go, I felt somewhat privileged. Because of my work at the Austin Center I personally knew some of the chaplains, including Carlos Craveiro. Carlos was free to move about the prison at will. On the second night in my new residence, he visited me at 11:30 P.M., bringing books and letters. I was a prisoner, but I relished the familiar feeling of being one of "God's kids." I felt special.

I felt the brush of privilege again one night when Carlos stopped by at about 10 o'clock. He gave me a few letters and some pictures of Lois and the kids. But he also brought some bad news. He told me that he believed God had spoken to him about granting me special treatment; this would be his last visit after-hours. I protested, "I've been here for a week. Twice in a week is not too much." I was trying to hang on. It did no good. God was prodding me to let go and to face Him alone.

God was also challenging me to forsake my selfish desires. But selfishness is instinctive for people who are in pain, and pain dominated my life. It was deep and relentless, like a huge crevice that nothing could fill short of my being restored to freedom and reunited with my family. On the other side of the wall, Lois was experiencing this same feeling. She wrote in her diary, "Emotionally, the hurt is always there—a deep hole, a bleeding ache—deep inside."

In those first few days, my energy level was almost nonexistent. I pulled myself through each moment only with great effort. I felt broken down, empty before God. Even then, God was calling me to let go. My long journey of growth was about to begin.

One challenge to let go came on a Tuesday night, the night on which there was a division-wide Bible study in the chapel. So many had come out for the study that the prison ministry group, familiar with my background, asked me to lead a group of about twenty men. My first reaction was to decline. Earlier in the day God's Word had exhorted me to trust and not fear. But I could not help but fear. My heart ached with fear. I simply could not find the strength to stand up before others to lift their spirits when my own spirit felt pierced through.

Yet I had been trained to regard ministry as a duty. So I accepted. The passage for that night was 1 Peter 1:6-8: "In this you greatly rejoice, though now for a little while you may have had to suffer grief in all kinds of trials. These have come so that your faith . . . may be proved genuine and may result in praise, glory and honor when Jesus Christ is revealed. Though you have not seen him, you love him."

As I choked my way through the final words of that passage, I realized that there is a profound difference between loving God and loving to do ministry. A verse from John 21 came to mind: "Do you truly love me more than these?" *How much do I truly love my Savior?* I thought. *And how much do I merely love ministry?* Six men asked Christ to come into their lives that night. This was good news to report on the fruits of my newfound prison ministry, but I knew that such "success" meant nothing as far as my life was concerned if my own spirit was not right with God.

I returned to my cell with an understanding of what was lacking in my spiritual life. But this new understanding did not constitute the end of a journey; it was only the beginning. I confessed to myself that I, like so many believers, did not truly want more of Christ, but only more of what Christ could give. In fact, there was only one thing I wanted: to have the door to my cell fly open and hear the guard call my name and say that a mistake had been made. I wanted my life to be the way it was before.

And so I resorted to prayer, the kind modeled after the widow in Jesus' parable of the unjust judge. She prayed until she got what she wanted. I resolved to assail Heaven with my prayers until I got what I wanted. I realized later that even prayer is misguided when the primary motivation is to fulfill personal desires rather than to seek Christ.

Knowing what we should do and how we should pray, to the Christian, is just the beginning. I "knew" that seeking Christ should be above all else. But that message had only begun to touch my spirit, which was still weak. Growth does not come with mere knowledge.

A speaker at a Full Gospel Businessmen's Association meeting once posed the question, Can you eat ravenously from the Master's Banquet Table without a thought for those who have never eaten?

That was me. I began to realize I had a bad case of table manners. I had been like a pig, eating gluttonously every day from the good things the Lord had put on my plate, with little regard for the Master of the feast or for what He desired in my life.

Though Carlos had determined to cut back on his visits, he had not left me unarmed. He'd left with me a copy of *The Imitation of Christ*. In it, Thomas à Kempis combines Scripture with personal meditation for the sole purpose of separating the believer's heart from the world in order to offer it up pure before Christ. I'd had opportunities to read this book before, and in fact had read it some. I'd always put it down before long, finding it too hard to take.

But now it became spiritual sustenance for me. I expected it to search me; instead it tore me apart, holding the clearest of glass to my very soul. I could not escape the metaphor of the hand grasping the things of this world.

I began to confess, bent over in my cell, that I had been seeking not more of Christ but more of his benefits: my wife, my children, my freedom. God was showing me who I truly was, while at the same time revealing to me who He wanted me to be. As I realized the immense gap between the two, I wept.

I began to make a conscious effort to give up gifts I had long enjoyed from God. I embarked on an intense period of fasting and prayer, losing thirty-five pounds over the next three weeks. Once, having fasted for three days, I received my tray of food and began to thank God for it. The thought crossed my mind that perhaps I loved this food more than I loved God. I pushed the tray away and resolved to fast through yet another mealtime.

I do not mention this here to imply that people who have never fasted are unspiritual, or even that fasting or any other spiritual discipline must necessarily be a part of a Christian's spiritual walk. However, I do believe that for all Christians, certain times in our lives are sacrosanct, set aside by God in order to accomplish His unique will for our lives. I was in the midst of such a time.

One of the purposes for which God used this time was to convict me—for the first time—about the way I had been treating Lois. I had possessed a pretty high view of myself—of my leadership abilities and what I thought was mature spiritual judgment. I reflected on instances in which I had belittled Lois, even in public.

Now, during this time when I was helpless and needy, feeling useless and totally at the mercy of others, Lois was amazing me. She was raising support for my legal defense and searching for a lawyer. She was taking care of the children and answering endless phone calls from people who wanted updates on the situation. God seemed to be holding her up to me and saying, "Behold my servant."

People who came to visit me told me that not only was Lois doing well, but she was filled with God's Spirit and was regularly encouraging friends who had called to encourage her. Lois herself told me that at times she felt guided by supernatural strength. I had always felt that my many put-downs of Lois were harmless jokes. Now I was realizing that they represented an attitude of superiority and arrogance. No one had ever corrected me for these inconsiderate statements. They'd left it up to God. And God was definitely getting the job done.

With each new spiritual insight or self-understanding, I instinctively thought that God had finally accomplished His purposes and it was time for my season of trial to end and for life as I had known it to resume. Little did I realize how far I had to go. Yes, I had learned some things about myself and about what God desired. But becoming a new person, as I would learn, goes far beyond propositional statements of truth that can be set forth in a three-point sermon or gospel tract. After so many times of thinking I had finally arrived, I would one day give up thinking that I could ever arrive at the place where God wanted me to be. Perhaps that is the place where true growth begins.

Though I didn't know it at the time, I was far, far away from that place. God tested me in many ways, including through minor disappointments. I cherished, for example, my weekly visit with Lois. (I was not allowed to see the children at all.) The rules said the visits could last for fifteen minutes, but for the first three weeks they went on for an hour; the guards apparently didn't mind.

One visit was particularly special, because we were approaching Christmas. I will never forget how especially beautiful Lois looked to me that day. After the allotted fifteen minutes, a guard approached me and told me it was time to return to my cell. I was angry, but I was also powerless. The small oases in my desert experience could dry up in an instant. I was still learning that there was nothing in this world—absolutely nothing—I could take for granted. I still approached the Master's Banquet Table out of selfishness, not out of love. I had a lot to learn, a long way to go to improve my table manners.

As I strove to apply the lessons I was learning, God was active on the outside as well. Gaius Berg, a young executive who was active in the futures business, heard about my situation at his church one Sunday. He'd recently perceived that God was calling him into some sort of work with the prison system or prison inmates, and as soon as he heard about my plight, he became convinced that he should become involved.

His partner, Joe Ritchie, also took an immediate interest in the case upon hearing about it from Gaius. Over the years Joe ended up becoming one of my most trusted friends and counselors, as later chapters will reveal. Not that he expects anything, but it would be impossible for Lois and me to repay Joe for all he has done for us.

By the time Joe and Gaius got involved, Lois and my father had already chosen an attorney, Arthur O'Donnell, who assured them he could win this case. He said he'd take the case for $10,000, which Lois and I regarded as a preposterous amount. But she'd done some shopping around. She'd gotten estimates ranging from $5,000 to $30,000. She realized, of course, that the cost might reflect in part the service we could expect to receive. But the reality was, we had no idea where the money would come from. In any case, she came to believe that ten grand was a bargain.

In fact, it may have been too much of a bargain. Had we anticipated the full range of possibilities within a criminal justice system loaded with inefficiency and corruption, we certainly would have shopped a little longer, for freedom has no price tag.

In early January of 1983, only a week or so after hearing about the case, Joe and Gaius offered to put up the bond money of $45,000. But Mr. O'Donnell discouraged them from doing so. Apparently O'Donnell felt the bond had been set too high, and he regarded it a personal challenge to get it reduced. Fortunately, after a few days Joe and Gaius went ahead with it anyway, informing Mr. O'Donnell that his objection was being overruled.

For Lois and me to come up with that kind of money was unthinkable. But God had revealed His power, miraculously touching the hearts of two men who barely knew me but were convinced about what they should do.

After Joe and Gaius posted the $45,000 in bond money, I left the Cook County Jail, thankful for what God had shown me and hoping that my experience there would be a mere blip on the screen of my life. But that was not to be.

5

When God Says, "Wait"

Second to suffering, waiting may be the greatest teacher and trainer in godliness, maturity, and genuine spirituality most of us ever encounter.

Richard Hendrix

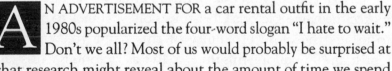

AN ADVERTISEMENT FOR a car rental outfit in the early 1980s popularized the four-word slogan "I hate to wait." Don't we all? Most of us would probably be surprised at what research might reveal about the amount of time we spend in life just waiting.

At the doctor's office, we wait. At toll booths, amusement parks, banks, grocery stores, and music concerts, we wait. And sometimes we must wait on God.

We pray for an end to racism and injustice, for hunger to cease among children, and we wait. We pray for healing, for wisdom, for guidance, for answers. And sometimes the only answer we receive from God is, "Wait."

Waiting on God is hard work. Many would rather face suffering than wait, which is to say that waiting is itself a form of suffering. Waiting implies confusion and uncertainty, when most of us would rather have things settled quickly. We want to know what it is we are up against, however bad, so we can decide what course of action to take and get on with life. Waiting frustrates those desires. It requires us to face the unknown. It tests our faith.

But waiting has a positive dimension as well. A child's anticipation of Christmas morning is a joyful kind of waiting. We look forward to weddings, family vacations, and other happy events with an excitement that often exceeds the excitement of the event itself.

Among life's most joyful kinds of waiting is looking forward to the birth of a child. In the summer of 1981, Lois became pregnant. Thus, in the eighteen months that stood between my release from jail and the beginning of my trial, we experienced, simultaneously, both kinds of waiting—the good and the bad, the exciting and the miserable.

Convinced early on that our third child would be a girl, we picked the name Victoria Christine. Lois was quick to point out to others the close proximity of this name to "Victorious Christian." But during this time, to live as victorious Christians was more of a goal for us than a reality. Waiting would take its toll on our lives.

I came out of prison determined to take another shot at successful Christian living. Through those many hours of prayer, fasting, and seeking the Lord, I felt spiritually rejuvenated.

I kept reading Thomas à Kempis in my devotions, making a conscious effort not to let anything, even Christian endeavors, take precedence over my relationship with Christ.

Another resource I leaned on during this time was the devotional *Streams in the Desert* by Mrs. Charles E. Cowman. My diary entry dated January 25, 1981—three weeks after being released on bond—was inspired by Cowman's book: "Trials are pointers to focus our attention on the lessons learned," I wrote. "God has, for the last few days, been teaching me lessons and showing me the purpose of trials: to better trust. It has been encouraging to see God steadily in control of things and for Him to confirm this trial as a training period from His hand. No other trial would have gotten my attention, forced me to listen, or caused me to switch roles with my wife, to be able to sympathize with her, to see her side of things."

During this time I began to grow in my understanding of the reality and true nature of spiritual warfare. I returned, frequently, to a scene from one of my favorite pieces of literature, J. R. R. Tolkien's *Lord of the Rings*. Frodo, the protagonist, had been growing in his awareness of spiritual realities. Through the use of a magical ring, he is better able to perceive the forces of evil that surround him. At one point he is under attack by these forces, represented as riders cloaked in black atop coal-black horses.

After slipping the ring onto his finger, Frodo can see fully the evil essence of his attackers. But he also sees a seemingly innocuous wood elf transformed into a powerful defender, a brilliant light with a shining white sword, who blinds the eyes and strikes fear into the hearts of the evil attackers.

I realized that I, by virtue of my faith in Christ, had the potential to shine like that transformed elf, like a bright light in the midst of dark demonic forces that I need not fear. For I was a child of God. This realization was a glimpse of what was possible. Knowing this and living it were two different things. After all, this concept of my identity still stood in conflict with what I had been taught—namely that, though saved by grace, I was essentially a sinner. This conflict was a long way from resolution.

I kept close track of the lessons I'd learned, searching diligently for God's purposes behind my suffering. My experience in prison enabled me to see Lois with new eyes. She was far more competent than I realized. For six weeks she had fought through her emotions to provide care for two young children and her incarcerated spouse.

In addition, God had challenged me to reevaluate my motivation for studying Scripture. There was a time when I studied the Bible simply to learn how to win arguments against those who questioned or challenged my beliefs. This is not necessarily wrong, but in my case the motive had been to increase my standing among others. I took great pride in answering people's questions. I recalled having thought that the Christian life was not so hard, that truth was easy to ascertain, that there was no situation I could not handle, no question I could not answer.

God challenged this "wisdom" in the same way he challenged Job, asking rhetorically, "Who is this who darkens my counsel with words without knowledge?"

Often, it seemed, I lived on the precipice of some new understanding of God, as if there was something He wanted me to learn, but it was just out of reach.

One thing that stood out, however, was my discovery of the true motivation for Christian living: to seek to know and love the Giver instead of to dwell on and expect the gifts.

Despite everything I was learning about what God wanted from me, the waiting made this a difficult time. We thought it would be a few months at most for the trial to begin. That did not happen. With my life in limbo as it was, I was hesitant to take a job, and we couldn't afford for me to return to school. So Lois went to work as a nurse, becoming the main breadwinner, while I watched the children and managed the Austin Center.

I was fully aware that if another murder took place in the

area, I would be an instant suspect. So I kept a log of my days' events as a reference. On nights when Lois was working, I made sure one of our friends came over to stay with us. In short, the situation, though on hold, still dominated our lives.

During this time we had an amazing outpouring of support from friends, especially those from our church, River Forest Bible Chapel, which established the Linscott Defense Fund to help pay the legal bills. A small group of seven also formed an investigative committee to help Mr. O'Donnell uncover clues, particularly with regard to possible suspects.

I also did what I could to help myself, taking a polygraph test on April 8, 1981, despite the realization that the results would be inadmissible in court. The man who administered the test asked me all the relevant questions, including whether I'd ever been in Karen Phillips's apartment. There was no question in the mind of the expert who gave me the test that I was telling the truth.

The summer of '81 came and went. With no sign of the trial in sight, I got a temporary job at a local Holiday Inn reservation center. When that was over, I worked at other short-term jobs. I'd long since quit writing in my diary, but I turned to it again on October 7 in anger and discouragement. I learned on that day that my own attorney was delaying the trial until at least the end of November. Something had come up in another of his cases. More waiting.

Two days later, on October 9, I slept in, a rarity for me. It was 8:30 in the morning. Lois had gotten the kids up and running; they were whispering so as not to disturb me. In that hazy ground between sleep and consciousness, I imagined them saying, "Who is that sleeping in there? Is that my daddy?" I'd been dreaming that this was my first night home after several years in prison. Obviously, despite our confidence in a positive outcome, the trial was deeply on my mind.

Our feelings, our perceptions of what God would have us know, and the messages we received from friends during that time were all mixed. On the one hand, we strongly believed that the trial would reveal the true facts of this case and that those facts were on our side. Yet my heart was extremely troubled. I had a sense of foreboding I could not shake.

Most of our friends encouraged us, assuring us that God was faithful and would never allow me to be found guilty. But one night we met with Mariyen Baisley, a missionary who'd gone out from our church twenty-five years previously and was back on her first furlough.

At our house for dinner, she shared with us some of the amazing adventures she'd endured in her time in Africa. She told of being taken away by soldiers, along with several other missionaries, to a secure compound for almost a year. Typically the soldiers would haul some of the women off for a night of use.

Mariyen recalled counseling a young missionary from Ireland, a beautiful red-haired woman who said she thought she would die if they ever came for her. One night they did. But she later reported to Mariyen that God had given her the help and strength she needed to live beyond her ordeal. As Lois and I listened, part of our hearts thrilled at the testimonies to God's faithfulness. And yet Mariyen's message for us was both clear and sobering: God's faithfulness to us was not contingent on my being found not guilty.

This same sort of mixed message dominated an amazing vision that came to me several times during the pre-trial period. It was a vision of Christ on a throne, smiling at me. His countenance was peaceful, comforting. I sensed His love for and patience with me during this testing period. His message for me in this vision was clear: "I'm not through with you yet." Despite these seemingly threatening words, I could not be afraid because of my overpowering sense of His abiding love.

This vision stayed on my mind and moved me for days. My response to it, however, left much to be desired. I did not ask what it was that I needed to learn. I did not want to know. Throughout most of my six weeks in prison, I had prayed for freedom, not for wisdom and growth. Frustrated with the waiting, and convinced I'd suffered enough, I had returned to that point. Despite the vision, my deepest desire was to be free of this intrusion on my life so that I could follow my original intended course.

I remember an elder at our church who mentioned once that when he got to the words "bend me, mold me, break me" in one particular hymn, he stopped singing. Why take the risk? he felt. Now I felt the same way.

In the midst of all the mixed messages and the uncertainty about where God was taking us, Lois's pregnancy took on symbolic significance. Especially since we'd been using contraceptives, we believed that God would not have allowed her to get pregnant if a prison term was in my future. One morning we together discovered a verse from Isaiah 66: "Do I bring to the moment of birth and not give delivery?"

The Lord, we believed, was perfecting our unborn daughter during the delay. With each day we waited for our new child, God was enabling her, perfecting her until the time was right for us to meet her. Likewise, despite backsliding with regard to certain truths, God was perfecting us as well: teaching us patience, keeping our eyes focused on Him.

The months wore on into 1982. The frustrations of the final days of Lois's pregnancy paralleled our frustrations with the legal system. We trekked to the hospital for four false alarms before Lois finally was ready to deliver.

Finally on January 28 at about 3 A.M. she went into labor. Soon afterwards we compared the pain of her labor to the pain of our experience. During one contraction Lois pushed so hard she popped blood vessels in both of her eyes. The doctor told her to let up a little.

At 7 in the morning, Victoria Christine was born. The months of morning sickness and discomfort, as well as the intense pain of those last hours, were overcome, instantly forgotten in the shadow of the joy of new life.

We anticipated also experiencing soon a joyful celebration of the end of my ordeal. Despite the warnings we had received from one source or another, we made plans to pack our bags and head back to Maine as soon as the trial was over.

Had we gone to trial a year earlier, perhaps we would have been more willing, more able to face all the possibilities. But waiting had taken its toll. We simply wanted this chapter of our lives to end so much that we listened, uncritically, to the promises of victory. Today I believe that our adversary, the Devil, used this time to test my faith, employing the hope of release to set me up for future disappointment. But God, who is more powerful, used the Devil to accomplish His purposes.

Our faith would be tested further, and it would bend in the heat of tribulation. God was not through with me yet. The metaphor of Lois's pregnancy still applied. God was still perfecting me, His child, through the labor of pain and disappointment. Bringing forth a baby takes time. And though I didn't know it then, I had a long way to go.

6

Judgment Day

"Then he isn't safe?" said Lucy. "Safe?" said Mr. Beaver; "don't you hear what Mrs. Beaver tells you? Who said anything about safe? 'Course he isn't safe. But he's good. He's the King, I tell you."

C. S. Lewis, *The Lion, the Witch and the Wardrobe*

SITTING THROUGH MY TRIAL was the most frustrating and anxiety-filled experience I have ever had to endure. I could not conceive of how what should have been one short, innocuous phone call could lead to this. In some ways it was hard to take the whole thing seriously. On the other hand, we realized what was at stake: my freedom and perhaps even my life.

Our frustration is illustrated in part by our mixed emotions surrounding the parents of Karen Phillips. While dozens of people attended the trial on our behalf—showing their support—Mr. and Mrs. Phillips sat alone. We knew it must be torture for them to relive the violent death of their daughter.

They believed I was guilty, partly because they needed to believe it. Putting the assailant behind bars might take the edge off their pain, and at the time I represented their best hopes of accomplishing that.

Had I grown up next-door to them or had they been friends of the family, they would have known I was innocent. We had no way of communicating that to them.

Nor could we speak with the prosecutors, despite our instincts to get to know them a little, to invite them over to dinner so they could see for themselves that there was no way I could have committed this crime. But the situation had progressed far beyond that. In an adversarial, impersonal justice system, they were my main adversaries. Whether or not we liked the system, we had no choice but to play by its rules.

As the trial progressed, it was clear that our battle was not against men, but against principalities and powers. Perhaps we failed to grasp fully the toll evil can take on the truth, on justice, and even on plain common sense. Clearly we were in the midst of spiritual warfare. In fact, I find it virtually impossible to understand and interpret the events that transpired except in terms of spiritual warfare.

At various points throughout the trial, Psalm 56:5 came to mind: "All day long they twist my words; they are always plotting to harm me." After the attorneys' closing arguments, but before I was pronounced guilty of murder, I remember thinking of the many things that should have been said but weren't. Through one technicality or another, or because of trial irregularities or questionable strategy on our part, the jury, I feared, had a completely misguided impression of what had actually happened.

❦

After jury selection, the trial began on May 27, 1982, with Judge Adam Stillo presiding and assistant state's attorney Jay Magnuson as the chief prosecutor. Stillo was the fourth judge appointed to the case. Mr. O'Donnell had objected to the first two based on their prior knowledge of the case. The third resigned after being diagnosed with a malignant tumor.

I was being tried for murder and rape. (A vaginal smear taken from the deceased contained semen.) The state's case consisted essentially of two elements: physical evidence (my blood and hair samples), which prosecutors argued implicated me as a suspect; and the dream, which they contended was not really a dream but a confession.

The physical evidence centered largely around analysis of the vaginal swab and on my status as a "non-secretor." A non-secretor is a person whose blood type cannot be determined by testing body fluids. The majority of the population—80 to 85 percent in fact—are "secretors." That is to say, they secrete small traces of blood into their body fluids: tears, saliva, and semen.

The state produced a forensic scientist who testified that only Karen's blood type was found in the vaginal swab. From that, the prosecutors incorrectly surmised that the killer must be within the 15 to 20 percent of the population who are non-secretors, in which I was included.

Another witness for the prosecution contended that, though not an exact science, it is possible to compare two hairs that had been separated from the same head in such a way as to conclude "within a reasonable degree of scientific certainty" that hair from a known source was "consistent with" that from an unknown source. The state's forensic scientist testified that my hair was "consistent with" hair samples found at the scene of the crime. And Magnuson told the jury that when a scientist says "consistent with," what he really means is "identical."

The heart of the prosecution's case, however, was something I'd provided: the dream. Magnuson drew out details from my written and spoken descriptions of the dream—he even surmised a few "facts" of his own—and molded them to fit the details of the actual crime, concluding that I knew details only the killer could have known.

Overall my attorney failed to challenge the state's case, although in fairness to O'Donnell, he was hampered by trial irregularities that went unaddressed and by a judge who, at each critical juncture, influenced the case against us.

O'Donnell pointed out that though many fingerprints were found in the apartment of the victim, mine were not among them. Also, despite the bloody nature of the murder, not even a hint of blood could be found on any of my clothes or in our apartment. Beyond that, about all O'Donnell could accomplish was to raise questions with regard to the shoddiness of the police investigation.

He emphasized my good record, producing character witnesses on my behalf. But Magnuson nullified all that in one fell swoop by comparing me with mass killer John Wayne Gacy and claiming that Gacy produced character witnesses at his trial, too.

As for the scientific evidence, O'Donnell never challenged the state's false contention that the vaginal swab evidence limited the pool of possible suspects to non-secretors, though he did point out that at least two or three of the jurors probably belonged to that pool.

O'Donnell also produced a forensic scientist who was both competent and convinced, based on the tests he had performed, that my hair did not match the hair samples found at the scene of the crime. Magnuson, however, questioned the reliability of our expert's methods and pointed out that the tests had been done hastily, less than twenty-four hours before our expert's testimony.

In my opinion, O'Donnell's biggest mistake was his decision

early on not to address the so-called "dream evidence." He simply urged the jury to disregard the dream, contending that it was irrelevant to the case. In other words, he wanted jurors simply to dismiss out of hand the state's contention that the dream was actually a thinly disguised confession. O'Donnell mentioned the dream at points throughout the trial. But in his opening and closing remarks he stated, "I don't know whether he [meaning me] had a dream or thought he had a dream. I don't think it is important in this case."

Unfortunately, the jury apparently did not care what my attorney thought was important. And that remark, I'm convinced, cast doubt upon my credibility and perhaps my mental stability in the eyes of the jurors.

When all the dust had settled, jurors had the following information on which to base their decision: They believed that blood tests placed me within a 15-20 percent segment of the population that could have committed the crime, and that hair bearing a close, if not an identical, resemblance to mine had been found at the scene of the crime. Plus, in the absence of any refutation, they likely concluded that my dream was a virtual carbon copy of the actual crime.

At that point only a few small holes tainted the prosecution's case. As mentioned, they had no fingerprints or blood. And they could establish no motive. Nor could they prove that I had ever met Karen Phillips, which carried some significance given the likelihood that she was murdered by someone she knew, as there were no signs of forced entry.

Perhaps the biggest hole in the state's case was the logic behind the theory that my retelling of the dream was a veiled confession. According to the theory that out of guilt I actually wanted to be discovered, I should have confessed to the crime when the police gave me the opportunity.

Nevertheless, the evidence seemed weighted against me. If that evidence was accurate, I suppose it would have been hard for me even to expect my friends to believe I had not committed the crime. The problem, however, was that the state's "facts" were not factual at all.

Take, for example, the evidence surrounding the vaginal smear. Since only Karen's blood type (Type O) was found, it sounds credible to presume that the assailant was a non-secretor. But the other possibility is that whoever had sex with Karen also had Type O blood, which is the most common type. This raises the pool of possible suspects from 15 percent to well over 50 percent of the population. This is something I feel O'Donnell should have caught.

The state had used a similar tactic when it came to the gamma marker tests on the vaginal swab. Gamma markers are genetic markers found in blood and other body fluids. All human beings possess twenty-five such markers identified by numbers. Only three or four are normally tested for forensic purposes.

According to the state's expert witness, Karen Phillips had gamma markers of +1, +2 and +10. As Gordon Haresign wrote in his 1986 book on this case, "When the body fluids of a rape victim and her assailant are mixed, the presence of plus markers in the victim masks the presence of plus *or* minus markers for those numerals in the suspect. Since the victim in this case had *all* plus markers, no male in the world could be eliminated as a suspect based on this test."

The state's witness testified that the test results were consistent with what he would expect if I were the assailant. Technically this was accurate, but it was also misleading. Had any male in the world had sex with Karen Phillips, the test results would have been no different. Yet, as previously mentioned, Magnuson, in his closing argument, contended that "consistent with" is a scientist's way of saying "identical." The state also made sure to point out that some of the tests had been done at Scotland Yard, which no doubt impressed the jury.

🦌

Understandably, things were tense around our place the morning of the final day of the trial. With my stomach in knots, I remember yelling sharply at Lois as I tied my tie for the tenth time, "Honey, where are my pressed pants for court?"

She responded, "I'm trying to get Katherine dressed. They're on the chair next to the bed. And stop screaming."

As I popped open a dresser drawer looking for socks, I noticed some new underwear Lois had bought for me. Suddenly I recalled some cheap advice a cellmate had given me back at Cook County. He said to wear three pairs of underwear the day the verdict comes down, just in case it's not a good one. I ignored the advice.

Lois and I, along with the three children, crammed into our tiny Mazda and rushed off to the baby-sitter's house. When we arrived I kissed each of the children while Lois gave instructions for their care. Confidently I told the baby-sitter I'd be back around noon. But as we drove away, I could not be sure when I would see my children again.

When we arrived at the courtroom, lots of people were flooding in, all of them being checked upon entry by court security. Reporters hung out near windowsills or around garbage cans so they could smoke before court began. Every now and then one of them would approach someone who was there on my behalf with a question. Finally the jury marched through on its way to the deliberation chamber.

One hour passed, then two. I was engaged in conversation with friends, my mind far away from the matter at hand until it was announced that the jury had reached a verdict. "This is it," I said to no one in particular as I made my way into the courtroom.

The judge read the verdict on both the charges and without expression handed the slip back to the court clerk. When the woman who announced the verdict proclaimed, "We, the jury, find the defendant, Steven Paul Linscott, not guilty of the offense of rape," Lois and I breathed a sigh of relief and whispered prayers of thanks to God. The next words she uttered, however, would send us reeling into shock: "We, the jury, find the defendant, Steven Paul Linscott, guilty of the offense of murder."

These seemingly incompatible conclusions testified to a confused jury. Because the vaginal swab evidence had played such a key role in the state's case, jurors most likely believed I'd had sex with Karen Phillips. Apparently they left open the possibility that the sex was consensual, despite no evidence that Karen and I had ever even seen each other. Or perhaps the mixed verdict was the jury's collective concession to its overall uncertainty, a way to ease the conscience by giving me at least some small benefit of the doubt.

In any case, the time for analysis was over. Within minutes I was in handcuffs. For both Lois and me, the first emotion was not pain but shock. The ridiculous had happened. I glanced over at Lois; she was expressionless. Both of us were temporarily numb.

My attorney had me sign a few papers related to the bond money, papers I would later regret signing. Two guards came and took me away to an anteroom. Lois was allowed to see me briefly. I held her hand tightly, trying to comfort her as best I could. But the reality was that little possibility of comfort existed in that moment.

The anesthetic effect of the shock faded fast as Lois began crying. Weakly she asked, "Where are they taking you?" But she already knew the answer. In less than an hour I'd be back in jail. I assured her that I would be okay, that God would protect me. As I handed her my wallet and my watch, the bailiff intervened. "Time to go, Mrs. Linscott," he said.

With that, we set out on separate paths of pain that would take years to join up again. What we thought God could never allow to happen had happened. And it would be up to us to seek Him as we embarked on separate paths of a common wilderness journey.

7

How the Impossible Happened

For without cause they have hidden their net for me in a pit, which they have dug without cause for my life.

Psalm 35:7, NKJV

ROM THE BEGINNING, those who had only sketchy details of the case displayed a hesitancy to conclude I was innocent, despite my Christian faith. But as people became more informed, doubts about my innocence faded away. The question that rose to the surface instead was, "How could this have possibly happened?"

My three-pronged explanation begins with the jury. As the quip goes, "How frightening that in courts of law our fates are determined by people who are not smart enough to get out of jury duty." Though a bit cruel, some truth is spoken in that jest.

For example, following the trial one juror said he was convinced I was a liar simply on the basis of my testimony that I had never met Karen Phillips. He apparently could not imagine me not knowing someone who lived two buildings away, even though Oak Park is a densely populated area and I'd lived at the Austin Center for only about a month.

This jury of my peers, I'm convinced, got caught up in the sensationalism of this case. After all, the script read like a made-for-TV movie. Even Scotland Yard was part of the story. Jurors' propensity for intrigue was evidenced in part by their discussion of newspaper clippings on the case, something prohibited by trial rules.

The prosecutors exploited every ounce of the drama. Magnuson argued, for example, that the victim, who was actively involved with the Temple Kriya Yoga in Chicago, had arranged her fingers on both hands to communicate a message at the time of her death. The arrangement of her fingers supposedly was a sign of peace and acceptance in accordance with the religious group in which Karen was active at the time. Magnuson's purpose was to link this with my statement, based on the dream, that the victim offered no resistance but had an air of acceptance or peace.

Long after the trial we became confident that while Karen's finger position was recognized in the teachings of the Temple Kriya Yoga, the position had nothing to do with peace or acceptance.

In any case, Karen had been severely beaten. Her skull had been fractured in more than one place. According to the coroner's report, gruesome as it was, pieces of her skull and brain were found on the rug. It is inevitable that she was unconscious long before the beating was through. To think that her fingers could have stayed in the same position through the remainder of the assault is unthinkable. If anything, the arrangement of her fingers should have implicated someone from the Temple, who would have known what he or she was doing. But it all sounded interesting, and in the absence of any effort to challenge these kinds of arguments, the jury apparently bought it all.

Improprieties during the trial also help explain how the jury reached the conclusion it did. One juror, against the rules, brought in the aforementioned newspaper clippings, one of which stated that I knew "details of the murder only the police were supposed to have known." Still another juror relayed information extraneous to the trial. All this came to light afterward through the sworn testimony of an alternate juror, who said she would have come forward during the trial but did not know she was allowed to approach the judge.

Other trial irregularities are attributable to Judge Stillo. He dismissed a juror who O'Donnell strongly sensed was skeptical of the state's arguments. The woman, a nurse, had to work one night during the trial and reported to the judge that she did not think she could stay awake. Typically cases are delayed in such instances, given all the time and effort both sides expend in agreeing on jurors. But O'Donnell's motion for a mistrial was flatly denied.

O'Donnell also argued that the state's evidence relative to the vaginal swab should have been disallowed since, according to the state, the swab had been consumed during testing. This denied us the opportunity to have it examined by our own forensic expert. Results of such tests might well have given jurors a totally different impression of the state's so-called "scientific" evidence. (Ten years later the state would inform us that the swab had not been totally consumed after all.) Stillo, however, refused to disallow the evidence.

The third explanation for the jury's verdict, as alluded to

above, is the strategy chosen by my lawyer. His decision not to address the dream entailed not preparing me to answer questions regarding the taped interviews. The first time I heard the tapes was during the trial. I had not read the transcripts for sixteen months. Thus when prosecutors questioned me, I seemed uncertain, unsure of myself, confused. I *seemed* uncertain because I was. Though I said nothing incriminating, my performance must have created an indelible, negative impression in the minds of jurors.

And when it was all said and done, impressions were all they had to go on. They did not have all the important facts and arguments laid out as neatly as they are here. It was all a big blur. No juror was qualified to make an intelligent judgment on the scientific evidence. None had the credentials to determine whose expert was more reliable. The state challenged the reality of my dream, presenting a theory that sounded convincing, especially in the absence of a response. Magnuson and his assistant were skilled orators, salesmen who could peddle ice cubes to Eskimos. The jurors were putty in their hands.

In time, both the Illinois Appellate Court and the Illinois Supreme Court would concur with our analysis of the trial and would conclude that I had been denied justice. They would agree with us that the state's supposedly factual evidence was neither factual nor evidence. They would say that Magnuson had engaged in "outright fabrications." According to the Illinois Appellate Court's ruling, "The prosecutor's misrepresentations relating to the hair and blood comparisons precluded any possibility of a fair trial." It continued, "Here the American ideals of fairness were not just ignored, they were trampled upon." But until that time would come, my family and I would have a lot to live through.

8

Back to Basics

In God's economy, a person must go down into the valley
of grief before he or she can scale the heights of spiritual
glory.

Billy Graham

THE HUMAN BODY is truly an amazing display of God's
handiwork. It tends, naturally, toward healing. When it
is cut, bleeding begins immediately to cleanse the
wound. The instant a bone is broken, it starts to grow back
together. Healing has begun, even though at first we experience
only the pain and trauma of the injury.

The same applies, I believe, to spiritual and emotional
injury, which I incurred the instant the word "guilty" rolled off
the clerk's tongue. Healing begins with tears, which signify
acceptance of the tragedy. Tears inform us that, technically, the
grieving process is on track. I say "technically" because in my
case the tears certainly did not bring with them any feelings
associated with being healed. At first, Lois and I, as well as our
friends and families, felt nothing but the pain of injury. Our
emotions were still on a downward spiral. The injury was running its course.

Lois and my dad left the court building together. Dad had done everything he could. He'd been there to support us through the trial, having mortgaged his home in Maine to help us with legal costs. It was a bright, beautiful, sunlit day, but the weather did nothing to lift their spirits. They embraced when they got to the car, then cried out a small portion of the pain. Their healing had begun.

They returned to the Austin Center and found our little, portable swimming pool in need of a cleaning. Lois pushed aside the tightness in her throat and the pain in her chest. She and Dad immediately went to work cleaning the pool. They were looking for something to do, a diversion. Lois told Katherine, who was five, that some "bad men told lies about Daddy and put him in a place where bad people go." That didn't mean she could not enjoy the swimming pool. Perhaps there was healing in that.

I was escorted from the courtroom to a subterranean lockup amidst a crush of convicts. Word quickly spread that "another Gacy" had just been convicted. Someone had apparently overheard Magnuson. A guard entered the lockup and screamed at me to come over to him. In summoning me, he used the name "John Wayne Gacy." I thought I might be in for one of those beatings that gets recorded as a fall in jail. Instead, he just stared me down for a few seconds, then walked away.

Then it was off to Cook County Jail, where I would remain until the judge handed down my sentence six months later. It was a Wednesday, the night our church held its usual midweek service, but Lois was too distraught to go. We learned that the service consisted of one act. There was no singing or praying or sharing. There was only weeping. Our friends were struggling with us and were healing in their own way.

One among them, Mariyen Baisley, did not weep. She

approached this situation from a different angle. Her years of experience on the mission field, experience that included many tragedies, enabled her to view my situation in the context of God's larger purposes. Mariyen came to visit me in jail that first week. As we talked, my eyes clouded up from time to time with tears, but she offered no sympathy. Instead, her face beamed with the joy of the Lord. I needed people to weep with me. But I also needed people like Mariyen to point me toward a kind of joy that rises above circumstances, toward a peace that defies understanding.

Dad visited me that first week. I could probably count on one hand the number of times I'd seen him cry up till that day. He does not cry easily. But this was not easy. Visiting one of the world's largest city jails makes an impression on any law-abiding citizen. Seeing that fortress knowing that his son would be confined there or in a similar institution, perhaps for twenty years or more, understandably tore Dad apart. How much more God must have grieved to see His Son suffer pain and humiliation for crimes He did not commit.

As Dad waited on the steps of the visiting area, a large, uniformed black man approached him, offering help. The man was the superintendent of the division. He gave Dad instructions on how to leave money for me. Dad was strengthened and encouraged by this small token of official concern. He would soon return—driving twenty-two hours straight—to the Maine woods to deal with his grief there.

The reality of my situation had still not sunk in totally, perhaps because we held out hope that bond would be granted. Mr. O'Donnell had led us to think this could happen, though we learned later that with murder convictions, the granting of bond is rare. Also, in those confused moments after the verdict was announced, he had gotten me to sign papers turning over control of the bond money to him. Six weeks later bond was denied. Mr. O'Donnell left town on vacation, keeping back some of the bond money for himself, fees he apparently thought he deserved. Our search for a new attorney began in earnest that day.

On the day bond was denied I was taking a nap. I woke up at about 3:30 in the afternoon and began to pray. I immediately had an overwhelming sense that the decision on bond had been made and that the news was not good.

Later that day I tried to call Lois, but she was not home. So I called a friend, Carol McClean. It fell on her to deliver the news. My first response was anger. Then I began to weep, overcome with fear and despair, the tools of the Devil.

This was something I simply could not accept. I'd concluded that since I had nothing to do with the crime, we simply had to win a bond. I was also convinced that this second go-round in Cook County Jail, a six-week period that seemed more like six years, was Job-like enough for all of us. God, I felt, simply could not allow this to continue.

My voice cracking, I said, "I cannot do another day here, Carol." She told me to try to call Lois that night at 7. When I did, I tried to be strong for Lois's sake. But the full reality of my circumstances, of my despair, was sinking in.

"Lois," I said, "I think I'm losing my mind." Fear and anxiety seemed to grip me as if they were living things. The Devil had been waiting for his chance to destroy me, and that chance had finally come. My mind and my spirit were reeling from the weeks of separation from my wife and children. At that moment I simply could not conceive of how I could take any more.

"Hold on, Steve, please. You've got to hold on," said Lois, weeping with me. "Please, honey. You've got to get ahold of yourself."

"I'm trying," I said, fighting tears. I had always been the strong one, but not now. The very thing that had been the source of my strength and confidence—my faith—was being swallowed up by despair. The Devil was so near, I could almost feel him.

As soon as Lois got off the phone, she called as many people as she could think of to pray for me. She was particularly intent on enlisting the support of prayer warriors who regarded spiritual warfare with the utmost seriousness. Among those she called was Dr. C. Fred Dickason, a theology professor at Moody Bible Institute, who specializes in studying and teaching about all-out war with the Devil.

Communicating through Lois, Dr. Dickason exhorted me to resist the Devil and not to give in. He encouraged me not to believe my thoughts and feelings, but to trust in the Lord instead. Perhaps most importantly, he himself began to intercede on my behalf.

About an hour after I got off the phone with Lois, this overpowering sense of oppression began to wane. I felt at least some sense of control returning, even though I was still depressed at the prospect of having to go to a penitentiary. I wept uncontrollably, fighting to hide my tears from the other men on the wing. I thought about praying but felt totally incapable.

At 9 P.M. I was returned to my locked cell, and I quickly fell asleep. No doubt gleeful for my suffering, the Devil was not through with me yet. That night I dreamed I'd lost my soul and gone to Hell. I could see and feel the flames. I dreamed I was screaming as I experienced the pain of knowing I was lost forever. The dream seemed incredibly real. I awoke in a cold sweat, exhausted and frightened. I was relieved to discover that it was just a dream. On the other hand, this forsaken place where I was confined was a kind of hell nevertheless.

The next morning my spirit was weak and in pain. I had been reading through the New Testament, but this morning I felt no stirring to continue. My spirit had been injured, assaulted. I was now experiencing the full force of that injury. Despite how I felt, I knew I should at least give God the chance to speak to me.

When the body is injured, it may take months or years for full healing to occur. An athlete who's had a knee reconstructed gets out of the cast to find his leg muscles withered away to half their normal size. That first day of rehabilitation consists of merely lifting the leg from the table.

The first steps of spiritual recovery are just as simple. I was not ready for any profound theological insights. My Bible was marked at the Lord's Prayer. Having been reared in the Catholic Church, I'd recited that prayer countless times as a child. And now here it was before me again. Surely, I could read it one more time. Just the Lord's Prayer, nothing else.

As I took this small, simple step of faith, strength began to seep back into me. That old, familiar passage, which I was reading again with a new set of eyes, breathed new life into me, giving me strength to go on and even to pray a little that day. I began to believe again that God was with me in that cell, that nothing could separate me from His love, that no matter how dark the valley or rough the way, God could and would somehow make it bearable. I would have preferred merely to read about God's faithfulness in tough times, but God was calling me to experience His faithfulness in the darkness.

I would need every ounce of strength, confidence, and wisdom to negotiate my way through six months in Cook County Jail's Division Six.

For a short time I was without a cellmate, or "celly," as we called them. Then a young man named Angelo, a Christian who was quite open about his faith, moved onto the wing. He'd taken some courses at a Bible college but was unable to deal with some problems dating to his childhood. He'd gradually slipped into a sinful (and illegal) lifestyle.

Angelo and I became cellies. His mood swings could be extreme and unpredictable. He was very uplifting in some of the "sermons" he preached to me, and the words "praise the Lord" were never far from his lips. But he would also get discouraged and depressed when something did not turn out as he'd hoped.

Angelo talked constantly, something that eventually got him into trouble. His chatter attracted the attention of a member of one of Chicago's most-feared street gangs, the Disciples of Satan. The general consensus was that this guy was mean and dangerous. I can still see his eyes rolling as he talked, reminding me of a watchdog, a Doberman, I saw chained to a fence during my Navy years in Guam. The sun had baked this canine's brain so that he'd snap at anything that came too close.

Angelo got too close, and one day this Disciples guy entered our cell and began pounding on Angelo. Angelo tried to cover up to shield himself from the blows. At one point he cupped the guy's face with one hand and had an open path to overpower him with the other. The bully's eyes widened in terror as he realized he was defenseless. But Angelo never threw the punch. Instead he covered up and was hit again and again.

When the guy landed one in Angelo's groin, I stepped in. "You've made your point," I said. "Angelo could have knocked you out, and you know it. He's not fighting back. You made your point." Then I grabbed the guy and threw him out of our cell.

Unknown to me, the rest of the wing had gathered outside our cell to observe the proceedings. I threw the guy into the waiting arms of some of his fellow gang friends, a dozen or so of them. Men who had been civil to that point now gazed at me with murder in their eyes.

The cell door was still open. They could have come in and killed both of us, and Angelo and I knew it. We stood with our hands at our sides, looking at them. In the courtroom I'd been overcome with fear. But in this situation, with my life in imminent danger, I experienced no fear at all. Instead I felt God's perfect peace.

The move was theirs to make. Amazingly, not one of them moved an inch. Perhaps they respected our determination to stand up to them. Whatever the human reason, it seemed to me that angels were blocking their path.

"I'm gonna get you, man," the attacker screamed at me. "It's personal now. I'm gonna get you." But not that day. The men cleared out. I realized in that moment how little provocation it would take for these guys to kill. Some of them were in for life anyway, so they had little left to lose. This made me aware that God had not abandoned me in this hellhole. He was with me, protecting me and granting me the courage and wisdom to survive.

The incident did not stop Angelo from carrying on with as much energy as before. He had a good voice and loved to sing. But he was too playful in an environment where most guys just wanted to be left alone. As a result he got on people's nerves. One night a gang leader who ruled the wing called out from his cell, "I want it quiet in here." Angelo kept right on singing and talking.

The next day, while I was attending a church service, the enforcer on the wing, a man known as Arkansas, showed up at our cell looking for Angelo. We knew the guy. In fact, we liked him. Angelo and I had discussed our faith with him, and he seemed close to becoming a Christian. Arkansas was gentle-spirited. If you teased him, he showed he could take it by laughing at himself. This laugh and his good humor camouflaged his huge chest and arms. This evening, however, Arkansas had a job to do, and that job was to punish Angelo.

After apologizing to Angelo, Arkansas proceeded to work him over. When I returned to the cell I saw Angelo lying on his bunk, battered all the way from his face to his knees. I was angry, but as I was about to seek out Arkansas, Angelo grabbed me by the arm. He told me that he'd forgiven Arkansas and had told him so after the beating. He made me promise to leave it alone. And I did. That night we prayed for Arkansas. A few days later he resigned from the gang, trusting God to protect him.

Arkansas was not around to protect me when the guy I'd thrown out of my cell approached me one day with a score to settle. I was sitting down out on the wing when he leaned over me. "I got to do this, Linscott," he said. "Take off the glasses." As I bolted up from the floor, I took a hard fist to the face as he broke glass against my head. I returned a karate kick to his mid-section, and he backed off. The "fight" was over. Noticing the commotion, the guards entered the wing and locked everyone up.

Angelo decided that things were getting a bit too hot on the wing, so he reported the fight. As a result, Angelo, the attacker, and I were placed in the segregation unit. The following day I was moved to another wing, overseen by a Christian guard.

❦

With all the excitement I was experiencing inside Cook County Jail, things were happening on the outside as well, thanks largely to the efforts of Gordon Haresign, a teacher at Emmaus and in some ways a mentor. Gordon's friendship and support during this time were immeasurable. He conducted his own private investigation, coming up with information and clues that would later prove helpful. He served as a contact person for people interested in the case, and he and his wife opened their home and their hearts to Lois and the children. Simply put, Gordon would not rest until he'd done all he could to help.

Joe Ritchie, who was as surprised as anyone with the guilty verdict, also rolled up his sleeves and went to work. He secured copies of the state's reports on the blood and hair evidence, and then spent countless hours in libraries trying to determine the significance of the state's tests. He talked with numerous forensic scientists in his focused effort to learn more. He asked each one of them who was the foremost expert in the field. As he worked his way up the ladder, everyone began to point in the direction of Brian Wraxall of the Serological Research Institute in California.

After Joe spoke with Wraxall about the case, there were two things Wraxall could not believe. First, he couldn't believe Joe had not trained as a scientist. Second, he could not believe what Joe was telling him about what the state had concluded from its tests. So Joe sent the materials out to California.

We ended up getting affidavits from both Wraxall and Edward T. Blake of Forensic Science Associates, also in California. Both of them went beyond saying that the vaginal swab evidence limited possible suspects to 55 percent of the population and said that the results of the tests performed by the prosecution's forensic scientist were totally meaningless.

In his affidavit, Blake contended that the analysis done by the state's expert "provides no more evidence against Linscott as the semen donor than it does against any other member of the male population." Wraxall drew the similar conclusion that "nobody can be eliminated as the semen donor" based on the state's tests.

Had this case ever gone to a second trial we would have argued that the state's hair evidence had been adequately refuted at the first trial, though the jury did not recognize it. The state had referred to a study concluding that the odds of two similar head hairs originating from different sources are 1 in 4,500. However, those odds are valid, according to the study, only if 23 characteristics of the hairs in question are compared. The state's expert testified at various points of the trial to having compared anywhere from 7 to 12. (At one point in the trial the state conceded that the 1 in 4,500 odds did not apply in my case, but in closing arguments Magnuson argued that they did apply.) In the first trial, our expert had testified that he was reasonably certain that hairs found at the scene of the crime could not be mine. The fact is that his tests are regarded among forensic scientists as being far more reliable than those performed by the state's expert. But, as mentioned, Magnuson succeeded in discrediting our expert's testimony.

Also, had we been given the opportunity at a second trial, we would have confronted the so-called "dream evidence" head-on instead of ignoring it. The jury was left with the impression that my dream was exactly like the crime when in fact there were major differences.

Determining similarities and differences was to some extent a matter of opinion. I said the assailant in my dream was about 5'6" tall, while my height is over six feet. The state considered that a similarity, but having played basketball with guys who are six inches shorter and six inches taller, I would beg to differ. In all we counted over seventy differences between my dream and what the state contended was the actual crime.

At one point the police had asked me if I noticed any "religious articles" in my dream. It was a leading question; there were many such articles in Karen's apartment. But I said no. My dream was distinct from the actual crime not just based on what was in it but also on what was missing.

The state claimed that I knew the weapon used to kill Karen was a tire iron, which had been found in the bushes outside. They said I'd used the words "tire iron" in my phone call prior to the taped questioning. But in the several hours of tape-recorded questioning, despite many opportunities, I never once described the weapon as a tire iron. My description of the murder weapon bore little resemblance to a tire iron, and the police never suggested on tape that I had earlier referred to a tire iron.

In addition, we had my dream analyzed by a highly regarded psychiatrist. Dr. Bernard Rubin of Chicago concluded that the dream, as I originally reported it, had "the qualities one usually associates with a dream." He said, for example, that my dream was vivid, but vague with respect to the details. He added that it is common for people to be awakened by dreams of anxiety and to return to the same dream story upon falling back to sleep.

In other words, if I were guilty, not only would I have had had to pull off the crime without leaving a clue, but I would have had to concoct an account of a dream and describe it in such a way as to fool an expert into thinking it was real.

Still another tack we'd planned to employ at a second trial was to point toward other possible suspects. Thousands of dollars were poured into investigations that produced at least five and as many as eight people who had the opportunity or motive to have committed this crime. The details of these investigations would make a fascinating book in their own right.

Various theories concerning what really happened the night Karen Phillips was killed account for such evidence as the presence of Negroid hairs at the scene of the crime. In addition, they consider the likelihood that the killer was an acquaintance of Karen's. Respect for libel laws, coupled with the fact that there is no "smoking gun," prevents the mentioning of any names or details here.

Joe, Lois, and Gordon interviewed several attorneys, most of whom seemed more interested in getting me freed on some technicality than in emphasizing the truth. None would allow us to work with them.

One exception was Thomas Decker, who was able quickly to absorb the complexities of the case and who had no doubt about my innocence. Mr. Decker prepared post-trial motions. These motions did not primarily address sentencing. Instead, he would argue that the evidence simply did not point to my guilt. His second argument was that, based on improprieties of the first trial, especially the prosecution's intentional misuse of evidence, I should be granted a new trial.

By then Mr. Decker was armed with the aforementioned affidavits Joe had secured, plus a statement from the alternate juror alleging trial improprieties. He also had two top-rate assistants in Richard McLeese and Jim Huston.

Tom argued that my rights to a fair trial were compromised when the state consumed physical evidence without our side having a chance to test it. Regarding the hair evidence, he cited a previous case in which a guilty verdict was reversed because a prosecutor had prejudiced the jury by saying that similar hairs should be regarded as identical. That was exactly what had happened in my case.

Not only did Tom bring out the facts of the case, but he also attacked the prosecutors, arguing that the state "knowingly used the truth falsely" and "encouraged the jury to believe what it knew to be untrue. . . ." Then he cited case history to establish that such breaches of conduct constitute grounds for a new trial.

I strongly believed that any neutral observer would regard those arguments as airtight. Apparently they seemed so to Magnuson, who spent most of his time not addressing any of our legal arguments, but attempting to justify his actions. When a man's freedom and perhaps his life are at stake, I simply could not conceive how it would not be enough at least to merit reexamination—that is, a new trial.

But the decision, unfortunately, was not left to a neutral observer, but to Judge Stillo. For him to grant a new trial might have implied that he had not done an adequate job the first time around. It would have taken a little bit of courage, perhaps more than he had. We may never know what all went into his decision-making process. We do know that Stillo himself, as of this writing, is awaiting a prison term, having been convicted of accepting bribes, though it is unknown whether bribes influenced his decision in my case.

All of Mr. Decker's months of thorough, painstaking research were nullified by a flip of Judge Stillo's hand. Mr. Decker was stunned . . . and furious. But I was not surprised. In those months I had grown close to the Giver. I strongly sensed God revealing to me that our attempts at that point for a new trial would be futile.

The night a new trial was denied, I made the following entry in my diary:

Complete bustout today. The State had nothing to offer to contest the motions. Judge just flipped a hand in the air and denied all three motions. He did all that I feared. (He was too afraid of the publicity to do anything.) Mr. Decker was angry and shocked. So was I. Judge Adam Stillo slithered out from under his responsibilities and conveniently let someone else make the decisions for him. Magnuson was all half-truths, lies, or wicked innuendo. We really did take the entire case away from the

State. There is nothing to prosecute with, no counter affidavits were even offered, so in effect they agreed with our findings. Magnuson looked nervous as usual these days, and even his voice broke a few times. . . . I only trust that God is still in control and that our lives are in His hand. I only wonder at the efforts He led us in to be disappointed. Well, God, only You know Your purposes in that. We knew our judge was useless from the beginning. Lois sounds encouraged in her faith, and I'm ever hopeful of good coming soon to us, though we now are preparing for a long separation and incarceration.

One of the things that hurt most when I considered a long prison term was the realization that I would be away from the children in what many consider to be the most enjoyable and the most important years of parenthood.

The day after the motion for a new trial was denied, I learned that Vicki, our littlest one, had fallen from a top bunk and cracked her skull. Lois spent the night with her in the hospital. I worried about Lois, knowing that she would blame herself for the accident. She was physically and emotionally exhausted and needed a night at the hospital just as much as Vicki.

Feeling helpless in these situations, I became angry. But sometimes anger helped me to focus my thoughts. On the night I heard about Vicki falling, I humbled myself before God. The influence of Thomas à Kempis was clearly evident in another of my diary entries. I wrote: "We actually are only creatures, and God is the Creator, so we on those grounds have no complaints. We do have added consolation and position in Christ, so that we are on a better footing than others."

Earlier in the day I had written, "Stillo may be stirred up to give me a long sentence after his face I saw yesterday, but that just makes the story more interesting. I'll only do the time that

God gives me to do. Hopefully my attitude will remain good towards the Lord, and my heart will remain fresh towards Him. I know that it is only His grace that keeps me calm and stable now, upheld and ever cheerful, at times mixed with little periods of depression."

As I look back on this period, I realize how important it was for me to understand and interpret my experiences through the lens of faith, even though my journey included periods of doubt. Many wrongly equate faith with belief. But belief in the reality of Christ and the truth of His promises is only one aspect of faith.

Faith, fundamentally, is a relationship of commitment. This commitment is easy to maintain when things are going well. At the beginning of a football game, when everyone is fresh and the prospect of victory lies ahead, confidence comes easy. But in the fourth quarter, when guys are tired and hurt and without a hope for victory, the true test of character begins.

Traditional marriage vows cover the gamut of circumstances. Whether richer or poorer or in sickness or health, the promise remains unaffected. The same is true of our relationship with Christ. To accept and follow Christ is a decision, a commitment influenced perhaps by emotion, but rooted in rationality and experience. It is a commitment that stands despite variations in feelings and life circumstances.

This relationship of commitment is strong enough to allow for feelings of anger. It is all right to be confused and frustrated, to have questions and doubts. The one thing we can't do is give up. We can't forget in the hard times the commitments made when life was better. And we hope that life will be better again. To some, such faith seems absurd. Why would I thank God for protecting me in jail, one might argue, when, if God really cared, He wouldn't have allowed me to go to jail in the first place? One could even go farther and ask, What good did faith do for those for whom God did not even provide protection? After all, even the strongest faith has not guaranteed that God's people would be spared martyrdom, death in a car accident, or starvation.

Whenever I doubted, I looked within and found Him stirring my soul. Maturity helps the Christian realize that faith is not influenced by circumstances, however dire. Instead, it entails a choice to understand those circumstances in the context of ultimate confidence in God.

In times of suffering or grief, we cannot deny that our faith is tested. It can be hard to see through our pain to a God of love. In these times, the choice to believe that God is in control can be difficult.

But I have found that God honors our efforts to seek Him and obey Him, even when we don't feel like it. The athlete who is recovering from injury at first can only lift his leg. Next time he can lift a few pounds, then a few more pounds. Before long, he's walking again, then running and leaping as before.

When our spirits are crushed or worn-out, God honors any effort we can muster to seek Him, to maintain the relationship, keeping the commitment even in the midst of our suffering. The body tends toward healing if we give it half the chance. And so does the spirit.

9

In the Lions' Den

Do not weigh highly who may be for you or against you. But take thought and care that God be with you in everything you do. Have a good conscience, and God will defend you well. For him whom God has willed to aid, no perverseness of man will be able to harm.

Thomas à Kempis

MOST PEOPLE who've never been incarcerated don't realize there is a difference between a jail and a prison. In most states, jails function as temporary holding cells convicts pass through until they are sentenced and assigned to a more permanent place of residence.

In general, prisons are more stable, and prison life is more routine. Jails are filled with guys who are fresh off the street and full of anger and energy. Freedom of movement is more limited, the guards are more brutal, and tension runs high.

One cannot underestimate the effect incarceration has on a person's emotions and his attitudes toward others. Receiving death threats almost every night, as I did at times in Division I at Cook County, tends to change one's outlook on life.

Near the end of my stay there, one of the guards called me into her watchpost to ask me if I was having trouble with any of the other inmates. I told her it was nothing I couldn't handle.

She had witnessed a recent incident of which I was unaware.

Lois had been in for a "visit" (if a conversation on opposite sides of heavy steel mesh can be considered a visit). When I was called away for a short time, a bunch of guys harassed Lois with verbal obscenities until they saw me returning. Lois did not say anything about it.

The guard offered to transfer me to another cell block, and I accepted. A day or so later, some officials called me in to tell me about the harassment incident. After hearing this, I was as angry as I have ever been in my life. I recall mentioning to one of the guards that I'd like to go back there and break a few chairs over a few heads.

One of them remarked, "They'd kill you," to which I replied, "They'd try. And I wouldn't care if they did."

My response was attributable in part to old-fashioned, rural values related to respect for one's spouse. But it also reflected how much my personality had changed, despite my Christian faith, in just a few months. I realized firsthand how ridiculous is the notion that our rehabilitative system rehabilitates. In some ways I had changed for the worse. I'd become reckless, emotionally numb, unconcerned about my well-being in the face of a possible lifetime behind bars.

They asked me to give them the names of three or four of the biggest troublemakers on the wing, which I did. I would learn later that this resulted in the formal placement of a "hit" on my life by the gang I mentioned earlier, the Disciples of Satan.

The date for my sentencing was set for November 23, 1982, and the opportunity to leave Cook County Jail would not be far behind. In cases with extenuating circumstances, murder convicts can get a life term or even the death penalty. More typically, they get from twenty to forty years.

On the day of the hearing, I got to see my children for the first time in over five months. Lois had dressed them up for the occasion. I will never forget how different but how beautiful they looked. As I held them, I could feel my emotions soar and sink all at once..

At the sentencing Lois testified to my faithfulness in our marriage and to my many friendships with others. She called me both her husband and her best friend, stating that nothing she had ever witnessed in my personality was consistent with committing murder. She closed by reading to me a Scripture passage from Isaiah.

I had trouble making it through my testimony. It was hard to make a case for a light sentence when I knew I deserved no sentence at all. During my testimony I made it clear that I was standing behind my claims of innocence, even while acknowledging that revisiting the question of my guilt or innocence was not on the agenda for the day. I affirmed my trust—and the trust of my wife, children, and brothers and sisters in the Lord—in God's love. I shouted as loudly as I could, "My God will deliver me."

But it was Judge Stillo who, at least on this day, would speak last: "I hereby sentence Steven Linscott to forty years in prison."

I returned to Cook County Jail to wait until there was room for me at Joliet. Two weeks later, the call to pack my bags came abruptly. Before most inmates were eating breakfast I was placed in a holding cell for big-time criminals. There were ten of us altogether. My forty-year sentence was light compared to several others whose sentences ranged from hundreds of years to life.

A maximum security institution, Joliet is essentially a pit stop for prisoners en route to a more permanent assignment. I knew I wouldn't be there long (it ended up being one month), but I would never have guessed my time there would be as eventful as it was.

As we waited in the holding cell, one man talked incessantly and mindlessly of "sweet drugs," girls, and bars. The ten of us, with sentences of forty years plus, looked on from inside our own special cage as the rest of the supposedly less dangerous criminals packed and dressed. Guards kept a close eye on us as we sat segregated from the hundreds of others awaiting transport.

We were held there until the other inmates had boarded the bus and a gate that would separate us from them was securely in place. Society is stratified even on a prison bus.

We waited inside this cage in the front of the bus for one more prisoner, an eighteen-year-old gang leader who'd been convicted of rape and murder and who had been in all the papers recently.

An older, Hispanic man grew impatient and started yelling at the driver and the guard as he kicked the cage with both feet. He stopped when the guard pointed a shotgun in his direction. The incessant talker I mentioned never stopped. His pace increased, and he grew more profane as he slipped in and out of reality.

I had the dubious distinction of being chained to the eighteen-year-old youth whose reputation for violence was widely known. Despite his tender age, this overachiever had climbed to the top of the gang world. He and his gang members had repeatedly raped a young woman and beaten to death her male friend at an elevated train stop in the city. He looked dangerous, even vicious, but after what I had just gone through, my emotions were numb, so I felt no fear.

All the publicity from his trial made him notorious. He'd helped sell a lot of newspapers. But his accomplishments notwithstanding, he faced confinement for life in a maximum security institution. At least I had hope. I can't imagine he had any.

He looked at me with hatred in his eyes. Unlike me, he had nothing to lose, nothing to prove. He could decide to beat on one more person and not be any worse off than he already was. I felt the need to say something. "I read about your trial," I said. "The press treated you pretty bad. I know what you must have gone through."

It was a feeble attempt to get on his good side. He turned away sharply and said nothing the whole trip to Joliet.

My memories of that trip are dominated by evil stares, faces frozen in fear, and blood-curdling hardness of heart. These were angry men who had taken that anger out on society. The guards were in charge, but they gave their orders from a safe distance.

When we arrived, doors of iron bars slid three feet to welcome us to our new home. We were herded by twos into the small concrete burrows.

Fortunately I did not have to share space with the eighteen-year-old. In the next cell, I heard him beat on his celly for hours as he demanded sex. "I've got a wife and three kids," I heard his cellmate say. The eighteen-year-old merely responded, "I don't see no wife here." Then I'd hear the dull sound of a fist striking against ribs until the poor celly finally submitted to sex.

If ever there was a time when I needed God's protection, it was now. I was surrounded by evil greater than any I had ever imagined. The cumulative effect of everything I'd been through in the last few days—the trauma of the sentencing and the savagery of living among high bond offenders at Cook County Jail—began to make an impact on my mental and emotional state. My anxiety was, of course, intensified by the fact that my future looked depressingly dim.

All the activity surrounding the move to Joliet had at least kept me from being introspective. But now I was alone without any friends, alone with no one I could trust, alone with my thoughts. Having time to think was harder than being active. I did not want to think about what was happening to me, but I was compelled to do so. Lying on my bunk, alone in my cell, I once more asked the question I'd asked from the beginning of this ordeal: "God, why?"

But there was no answer. Instead I heard the sounds of the two men struggling in the next cell, reminding me of the danger and perversity that surrounded me. I looked up at the fluorescent lights that buzzed from the ceiling and thought for a passing moment that they might be crickets I'd heard so many times on hot August nights in Maine.

Beneath me I felt the wetness of my pillow, which was becoming soaked with my own drool. The feelings of hopelessness—that nothing mattered and that I had nothing left to live for or care about—began to overtake me. I was on the brink of escaping into madness, and I tried to resist with what little strength remained within me.

"God," I prayed weakly, "in Your Word You've said that with every temptation You will provide a way of escape. Either that is true or You are a liar. If ever I needed You to help me, I need You now."

As soon as I prayed that prayer, I felt—very perceptibly—strength flow through me. The horror of my surroundings and the terror of what I had been through escaped my mind. Instead I was able to concentrate on the strength that at that moment was undergirding my emotions.

For several minutes I drew comfort and strength from a sweet, overwhelming feeling of peace. With this new strength I began praying for Lois. "Thank You, God," I prayed. "Give Lois the same help right at this moment. Help us both to sleep and rest." With that prayer I began nearly two days of restful sleep.

Of the 181 inmates on the bus to Joliet, I was the only one to be given a cell all to myself. The incessant talker from the bus went crazy after a few days at Joliet. A homosexual had caught his eye. One night when the cells were opened for suppertime, he charged the homosexual and began to maul him. The guards watched until the cell block had cleared, then separated the two. Such scenes I would learn to accept as commonplace.

At Joliet my life consisted almost totally of sleeping and reading. Our cells were opened only for mealtime. I yearned for new things to read. One day Bob Ramey, one of my professors at Emmaus Bible College, delivered to me an early Christmas gift. Inside a plain brown wrapper was a two-volume set—over 1,100 pages—on the life of George Whitefield.

I was particularly surprised by and delighted with this gift. I counted it among the many signs of God's presence, which He was revealing to Lois and me through His people. This made it easier, despite the circumstances, to have ultimate confidence in God's love and care.

Having so much reading material in some ways distinguished me from the rest of the men on the gallery. One blond-haired man—small but with the build of an athlete—approached me during a mealtime and asked what the books were about. After I told him, he proceeded, unprompted, to tell me about a man he had killed. He said he'd been pushing drugs and was cheated. So he went to the man's house and beat him to death with a tire iron. He said blood was splattered everywhere, that he was covered from head to toe. He then described how he'd disposed of the clothing at a friend's house.

I was appalled by the unsolicited recitation of this story, and it crossed my mind that this guy was a cop, a "plant." Perhaps the prosecution was maneuvering for a new trial already, or for a higher sentence. (I would later conclude he was not a plant.)

This incident brought me face to face with Proverbs 1, which deals with plotting the harm of another. This man had actually done something similar to what I was accused of doing. God showed me the heart of this man who was so eager for selfish gain that he regarded another man's life as nothing.

My walk as a Christian addressed such finer moral areas as dealing with pride and trying to grow closer to God. I could not conceive of how anyone could commit such a violent offense against another human being, much less plot that offense beforehand. How someone could do this was and is incomprehensible to me.

"How useless to spread a net in full view of all the birds!" Proverbs contends. "These men lie in wait for their own blood; they waylay only themselves! Such is the end of all who go after ill-gotten gain; it takes away the lives of those who get it" (1:17-19). I was struck again by the absurdity of my having been convicted of murder. These verses were not written about me.

This incident also testifies to what was happening to me in terms of my character development. I was becoming suspicious—paranoid—of everyone and everything. In prison, this is a survival instinct. I had no thought of the negative effects this would have on my life outside of prison, and I had no idea if or when that day would come. Once these walls are built up, they can be difficult to tear down. After I became convinced that this guy was not a plant, I lent him first one and later the second volume on Whitefield's life.

Unknown to me, on the outside Lois's high-energy state was getting her into trouble. She was so angry and disappointed at the injustice we had been dealt, she could not slow down or sit by idly. She felt obligated—driven—to act. From inside my cell,

I knew Lois was probably up to something, as she had always vented her emotions through constructive activity.

However, I had no idea of the extent of her activities. Lois was trying, singlehandedly, to prove the court system wrong. She was driving around town interviewing people, talking with anyone who might know something more about the crime for which I had been convicted. Dragging the children, including six-month-old Vicki, with her, she followed up on as many leads as was humanly possible for one woman in one day. She wore herself out and ended up in the hospital with a very high fever and pneumonia.

I was overcome with worry, my concern for Lois being heightened by my limited contact with people on the outside. After learning that she had been hospitalized, I went for four days before getting a follow-up report. It was then that I received repeated assurances that she was resting comfortably and improving. I considered that her hospitalization was perhaps God's intervention, His way of allowing Lois to rest and of telling her to slow down. In fact, I had been praying that Lois would find rest, and I considered this an answer to prayer.

After three days of being alone, I got a cellmate, a Christian who said he'd prayed to be matched with a fellow believer. We got along well and spent several days together encouraging one another in the faith.

The cell next to ours was inhabited by recent arrivals from Cook County Jail. One of them was an older, graying black man. The other, a younger man, talked well into the night of his many criminal exploits. I soon learned that this man—who went by the name Henderson—was afraid to sleep at night. Among the leaders of the infamous El Rukn street gang, Henderson held great sway over the lives of those in his organization. But he also feared being done in by a rival who was in the same business.

After two weeks at Joliet, my cellmate received word that he would be moving to the prison at Menard, another maximum security institution. He was transferred to a holding area to await space availability there, so I knew I was in line for a new celly.

A new shipment of prisoners was arriving, and workers were needed to help in the processing. I, along with several others on the wing, including Henderson, volunteered. After a long, busy day, I returned to my cell to await dinnertime. I was lying on my bunk when the cell door was electronically rolled back. My new celly had arrived. Lo and behold, it was Henderson.

Now, when you're in prison you don't expect to get Willard Scott as a cellmate. But to be paired with a high-ranking member of a dangerous street gang was about the worst thing that could have happened. I knew I was not popular among Henderson's fellow gang members. Apparently they'd decided that I did not fit the stereotype of a hard-core criminal. They called me "J. Edgar," implying that I must be a plant working for the FBI.

My relationship with Henderson had not exactly gotten off to a flying start. A week before he moved in with me, he'd heard me talking about my books on Whitefield and asked to borrow them. I explained that I'd lend them to him, but that somebody else had already asked to borrow them. That was not what he wanted to hear, and his response was threatening.

Tense myself from the environment, I'd retorted, "Hey, I'll lend them to anyone I want to." At the time I had no idea of the power this man wielded. That comment could have gotten me killed. Part of a gang leader's job description is never to show any sign of weakness, never to tolerate any threats to his power. And now we were roommates. I realized that I could very well be on his short list of things to take care of.

On our first night together, Henderson asked me, "Why did

the administration put me with you?" I was wondering the same thing and said I did not know. Henderson talked constantly, and he was very intimidating. He said he was a cousin of Jeff Fort, who was well-known in Chicago as the head honcho of the El Rukns.

Henderson told stories of how Fort maintained discipline over his gang members in prison. Once, Henderson said, when a gang member committed a mere minor infraction, Fort smashed the guy's head against the steel bars of his cell ten times. If he didn't have the presence of mind to swear allegiance after that, Henderson said, the man would be killed or at least carried out on a stretcher.

Henderson continued, claiming that a gang member had recently boasted that he could knock a man out with one punch. Henderson said the gang member would get his chance to prove his boast, and if he failed he would be disciplined. He told of the need to discipline another gang member who'd raped a white man at Cook County Jail, an act that went against the gang's rules.

He was not through yet, growing more obscene and sensational. He spoke of how white men would hire El Rukn gang members to have sex with their wives while they watched. He told of his control over one particular white family, of how he had sex with the willing wife and then proceeded to rob them. He talked also of a race war, envisioning the black race's complete domination over white society. And he boasted of various killings he had carried out or ordered performed in his presence.

How much of what he was telling me was true, I was not sure. I figured he was trying to determine if I really was an FBI agent, and if so to deal with me. In any case, my goal was simply to trust Christ and to try to witness to this lost and bitter man.

If his purpose was to intimidate me with all his stories, Henderson was succeeding. I told him point-blank that I felt intimidated and that I wanted this to stop. Figuring that he might be having a little fun before "wasting" me—like a cat plays with a mouse before killing him—I told Henderson that before I'd submit to any more intimidation, I'd "go out" like a kamikaze. He knew I meant it. It was a tense moment. He responded by saying it was not his intention to intimidate me. But I was not convinced. Neither was I convinced that, despite my faith in God, it was His will that I survive this prison experience. As far as I was concerned, my life hung on my cellmate's whim.

Each time I would leave the cell to meet with a counselor or visitor, gang members would call me "J. Edgar" when I returned. I distinctly remember my first visit with Lois since my arrival at Joliet. Not only did I meet with her, but I also spoke with Randy Frame, who helped me write this book but at the time was working on a news story for *Christianity Today* magazine.

Upon my return, the calls up and down the walkway rang out—"J. Edgar, J. Edgar"—from black faces pressed against prison bars. Henderson was tense and demanded to know where I'd been. After I told him, he said he wanted to know the make and model of my wife's car. Not knowing why he wanted this information or how he might be able to use it, I refused to tell him. Chow was in half an hour. Henderson said that tonight I was to come with him for dinner.

Nervously, I wondered if I had already eaten my last meal. For a few weeks I'd been saving salt packets from the chow hall. Now I took them and broke them open in my coat pocket. I have never been a violent person, but I have not been a pacifist either. If they attacked me on the way to the chow hall, I had a plan, though not much of one. I would wet my fist, dip it in the salt, strike whomever I could in the eye and leap over the rail to the ground floor three stories below.

As the cell door rolled open for chow, I listened closely for any sounds of running on the gangway but could hear none. Henderson conferred with passersby in low tones, but there was nothing unusual about that. Finally he looked back at me and said, "You coming?"

I got in step behind him, my goal being to keep at least two paces away from everyone, but particularly from clumps of men who might appear to have an ambush on their minds. At one point I let Henderson get several steps ahead of me. As I looked around and saw no guards, I got even more nervous.

When we got to the chow hall, however, there were guards everywhere. So far, so good. Henderson and I moved together into one of the ten lines filing through the chow hall. When we took our seats, I realized right away that I was surrounded by enforcer types from gangland, the best (which is to say, the worst) Chicago had to offer.

Henderson introduced me to the leaders of two of the city's largest black gangs. I was surrounded by meanness and muscle. Evil eyes were looking me over as I continued to wonder what Henderson had in mind. I simply ate my dinner and tried to be as pleasant as I could be.

The truth is, I was scared. I knew these guys could kill me in a heartbeat, and probably wanted to do just that. Had I truly been a police undercover agent, at that point I'd have fled for my life.

As I look back on that night, I think I know what Henderson was trying to accomplish. The conventional wisdom was that I was an administration plant. I suspect Henderson was taking some heat for not moving against me. He was trying to protect himself (and me) by having the others meet me and see for themselves that I was legitimate.

If that was indeed the plan, it worked. The others were apparently convinced I was who I said I was. One day Henderson told me he had a sister who lived in Oak Park and she had told him about my two-year legal battle and trial. He said it seemed inconceivable that the government would establish a relationship with someone so soon after prosecuting him for two years. Except for that, he said, he would have been convinced that I was a plant. Even so, he added, he was not so sure. But for the time being, I was getting the benefit of the doubt.

Not long after that, Henderson informed me that the Disciples of Satan had put out a hit on my life. He said they probably would have carried it out already, except for the fact that he was my cellmate.

My time at Joliet gave me a glimpse inside the world of gang culture. Henderson was a member of The Ruling 21, a sort of United Nations of Gangs. While gangs warred with one another on the streets, their leaders on the Ruling 21 made decisions regarding such things as turf disputes and gang activities. Because of Henderson's position, he would have to clear any effort to take out his cellmate.

Henderson explained that the reason for the hit was to get back at me for ratting on those guys back at Cook County. I told him my side of the story, essentially stating that I could take a lot, but that harassing my wife was where I drew the line. Apparently my explanation was good enough. After I was finished, I asked him if he was going to let the hit go through, and he said not to worry.

As time went on, we began to develop a respect for one another. Henderson became more willing to talk about the Bible and about Jesus Christ. I felt strongly that the Lord was working through me, at times guiding every word. What if the heart of a gang leader could be changed for Christ? Perhaps that is God's purpose, I thought, as I continued my search for answers as to why I was there.

One time Henderson shared with me about the religion of the El Rukns and their Moorish beginnings. I took that opportunity to provide him with one of the most powerful witnesses for Christ I have ever given. At one point he seemed to waver about becoming a Christian. He told me about having once attended church with his girlfriend (his pistol in tow). "I want to become a Christian," he said once, "but if I do, my own gang would kill me."

I responded by saying that I could not guarantee that God would protect him from death as a result of choosing to follow Him, adding, "But I can say that many have found death to be a small price for what Christ offers."

Just a few days after that conversation, I was transferred to the Centralia Correctional Center in downstate Illinois. This came as a surprise to many of those at Joliet who knew my story, since Centralia was a medium security prison.

Before I left, Henderson told me that he had arranged for my protection at Centralia. He assured me that I would start my next prison assignment with a clean slate, that permission to take me out had been denied. God's ways are mysterious indeed. He even transformed a dangerous gang leader into a shield on my behalf.

10

Light in the Darkness

Who could ever have thought that a soul, which seemed to be in the utmost misery, should ever find a happiness equal to this? Oh happy poverty, happy loss, happy nothingness, which gives no less than God Himself in His own immensity.

Madame Guyon

FALL HAS ALWAYS BEEN one of my favorite times of the year. In Maine, autumn was special partly because it was so short. The oaks, maples, and other hardwoods would transform into brilliant colors seemingly overnight, telling us all it was time to gather in the pumpkins and other garden harvest. The autumn air in Maine is like no other air I've ever breathed: crisp, fresh, and clear, filtered by the forest pines.

Each year at Thanksgiving our whole extended family would gather at my father's boyhood home, where my grandmother prepared an elaborate feast for seventy people. She had a special talent when it came to food. Her plump cinnamon rolls were legendary in that area. People made sure to pay her a call on baking day. She earned her living cooking for the leisurely wealthy in Bar Harbor.

It was in the fall of 1974 that I received Christ as my Savior, giving this season even greater significance. But eight years later, in the fall of 1982, I was sentenced to forty years in prison.

On paper, the December move from Joliet to Centralia Correctional Institute, from a maximum to a medium security institution, was a good one for me. But the reality was, I was merely going from one prison to another. My spirits were low for most of the trip downstate. When we arrived, I was unchained and uncuffed before being led into a one-story housing unit. After a brief orientation lecture I was taken to my new home—a single cell—and was handed new clothes, clean linen, towels, and my very own room key.

I had arrived just in time for the annual Christmas dinner, but I wasn't in much of a mood to eat anything. The inmate cooks had been allowed to prepare several special items to accompany the roast turkey and brown gravy. One of the inmates serving the food said, "God bless you" as he placed each portion on a plate. In that moment, despite my circumstances, I accepted his words as a true blessing from God. Though not like Grandmother's, this was truly a wonderful Christmas dinner. The Lord had missed no details. I was aware that He had not forgotten me.

Lois too was committed to never forgetting me. Although some of our friends had urged her to stay in Chicago, where she had networks of support, she had little trouble making the decision to follow me south. In September of 1980, we had read together the story of Adoniram Judson, the nineteenth-century missionary to Burma who was imprisoned for his faith. Judson's wife followed him wherever he was moved, camping just outside the prison walls. Inspired by that example, Lois would do the same.

On December 30 she, along with Bob and Judy Ramey, close friends of ours from Emmaus, came down to survey the lay of the land. In just one day she found a comfortable, safe, and affordable apartment for our family, a job as a nurse, baby-sitting, and a good idea about where to attend church. Indeed, God had not forgotten us.

A few weeks later Lois moved to Centralia. For the next three years she camped outside the prison walls. She never unpacked the boxes in her room, which was the smallest room in the apartment. She had no desire to unpack so long as I was a prisoner. To unpack, for Lois, suggested acceptance of a situation she refused to accept.

According to the rules, inmates may embrace their spouses only at the beginning and the end of a visit. However, when Lois came to see me for the first time in Centralia, the guards—against the rules—allowed us to curl up together with our arms around each other for almost the whole time. I do not know the reason this was allowed, apart from God's gracious provision.

Together we watched the snow fall softly on the prison yard beyond the bay windows. In my three and a half years of incarceration, this would be the only time the guards would bend the rules this far. But how we relished those moments on that wintry afternoon. Never again would I take for granted the opportunity to hold closely the woman I loved.

Despite the big picture, which was negative, we chose to interpret these short periods of grace as clear signs of God's presence. Instead of Papua New Guinea, God had given us a different kind of mission field. Bob Ramey encouraged us to view our situation as the school God had chosen for us. He admonished us to be faithful in our assignments, encouraging us to believe that God would always be faithful to us. Amid the darkness we longed for a time when the power of God's light would break through, and we believed it would come.

To possess such hope, however, does not diminish the pain of separation or the shock of incarceration. In the face of injustice, I felt powerless. In one diary entry in early 1983 I wrote that I considered myself "meat for the slaughter." To overcome feelings of hurt and disappointment, of being sidelined from God's service, was a daily challenge.

In a medium security institution, my concerns for my physical safety became somewhat less urgent. In fact, being accused of such an awful crime worked to my advantage. Since some inmates have jobs that give them access to prison records, there are no secrets about how long guys are in for and what they were accused of doing to get there. They knew that I'd received a forty-year sentence, quite long for a medium security prison. Knowing it was a weird case, some no doubt thought I was a psychopath. That was fine with me if it kept people from trying to push me around.

There was, however, no escaping the pure drudgery of prison life. "Laying up" or "laying in the cut" were common phrases among inmates, referring to hours at a time of doing nothing. It was easy to feel tired. There was little reason to garner any energy.

Some men, it seemed, tried to sleep away months at a time, while others tried to adopt routines to provide at least the appearance of meaningful existence. At Centralia my emotions had plenty of opportunity to catch up to the reality. When they did, I felt consumed with disappointment and anger. I had the virtually constant feeling that I was bleeding inside.

Not surprisingly, these feelings made the days longer than they might have been. They made living harder than it really was. They prevented me from counting my blessings. After all, as far as I could tell I was in some ways the most fortunate, cared-for inmate in the institution. I received scores of cards and letters, sometimes more in one day than most guys would get in an entire year. Lois never missed an opportunity to visit me. I even had a job that, by prison standards, paid well ($20 a month). Yes, I was in a tough situation. But the negative feelings of anger and disappointment only hurt my spirit more. I knew that somehow I had to get rid of them.

One morning I awoke with bitterness in my heart, feeling miserable and unable to shake the anger. I flipped on the little black-and-white TV Lois had sent me, and the first words I heard were, "I knew I had to forgive." The words were spoken by a woman who was a guest on "The 700 Club." I had the immediate feeling that I was about to receive a lesson from God.

The woman told of a camping trip she'd taken along with her husband and small children. Someone reached into the tent and abducted one of her daughters. The girl's body was found a few days later. She'd been raped and killed. I realized that what I was living through was a virtual vacation compared to what this woman had experienced. And yet she was able to forgive. And she testified that along with forgiveness she had received a certain measure of healing.

I quickly got off my bed and knelt down to pray. I did not feel like praying, nor did I feel like forgiving. This was a sheer act of will. In that moment God began to heal the pain in my heart and to bring peace. For me, the increase in my ability to forgive was a process, not something that came in a moment. But from that point on, as I began to pray more regularly for the power to forgive and to make learning to forgive a priority, I noticed a marked decrease in my feelings of anger and bitterness.

To the Christian, it only makes sense that this should happen, because our anger and bitterness is focused on those we regard as being responsible for those feelings. As we forgive, the focus of the anger begins to disappear. Warren Wiersbe has said, "The world's worst prison is the prison of an unforgiving heart." God, I came to realize, wanted me to forget about the people who were responsible for hurting me. For one thing, He would deal with each of them in His own way. For another, they had, after all, not done anything that He had not allowed. Focusing on my oppressors instead of on God had become a stumbling-block to my spiritual growth. And forgiveness was the way to get beyond that stumbling-block.

Preoccupied with the effort to understand and control my feelings, I found it difficult to concentrate on my job as a typist for one of the prison captains (high-ranking prison officials). My mind constantly wandered, finding its way to Maine and memories of my family. At times I could taste foods I'd eaten on the outside and vividly recall the feelings associated with certain activities. No one, at least, could take away my memories.

The stress was so much that I could not keep track of the paperwork, and so was eventually transferred to the gymnasium as a typist. I began a program of weightlifting and exercise, including tennis. This helped to fill the days with positive activity. One of the directors of physical programs took a liking to me; we played tennis frequently inside the gym.

Being in top physical shape would come in handy for me when a Hispanic gang leader and two of his buddies set out one day to do away with me. This guy absolutely hated the prison captain I'd worked for as a clerk. And the feeling was mutual. I'm sure he viewed wasting me merely as a way of getting back at my former boss.

One afternoon these three guys approached me as I was

alone working out in the gym. Their hand signals indicated their intention of clobbering me with a weight bar or free weights.

I'd been lifting pretty rigorously and had developed a fairly strong upper body. I didn't look particularly impressive until I pumped up with some arm curls, which is what I was doing as the guys began circling like buzzards, getting ever closer.

I had seventy-five pounds of weight on the bar as I went through my sets of repetitions. My plan was to save enough strength to swing it if any of them tried to move in for the kill. With three against one, they must have liked their chances. But they may have also realized that one of them might have some trouble waking up in the morning.

As I kept pumping away, I prayed to God for safety, but this time I prayed with my eyes open. Though I'm no Arnold Schwarzenegger, I could feel my muscles bulging out. One of them got a look at my biceps and pectorals all pumped up. He shook his head and walked away. A second guy did the same. Finally the ringleader stared me down for a few seconds before following his *compadres* out the door. I had a feeling of peace, a sense that God had performed a miracle. I'm convinced my biceps have never been as big as they were in my moment of need.

After a few months I learned of an opening for a religion writer at the prison newspaper. I regarded this as an opportunity from God to minister and took the job. Before long I began assisting in the newspaper's production and eventually became its editor. I drew encouragement from the fact that for the next few years our religion section, and the overall paper, regularly won awards in a competition judged by the Journalism Department at the University of Illinois.

Meanwhile, positive things were happening on the outside as various people worked to call attention to our plight.

E. L. "Al" Goss, interim pastor at First Baptist Church in Centralia, came to believe that the church was in great shape and that God had really called him there on behalf of the Linscotts.

What Al Goss meant to us during this time is perhaps best illustrated by the story told about a big storm that hit the coast of Maine. One family served as lighthouse keepers. The parents had to leave during the height of the storm to do their job. They told their little boy that God would take care of him till they returned. The boy replied, "But I want a God with skin on 'im." Al was born in Maine and still had his accent. He came to visit me often, to share information or a tear. He saw to it that Lois and the children received the care and support they needed. He was, to us, "God with skin on 'im."

The case had also begun to generate publicity. In February of 1983, *Christianity Today* published a thorough, well-researched account of the case, based largely on findings pertaining to the physical evidence that came out after the trial. The article, which appeared in the news section, was factual and was not intended to draw conclusions about my innocence or guilt. But after all, the facts were on my side, and so we used this article to inform and enlist others in the struggle.

Various Christian periodicals, as well as radio and TV shows, picked up on the article, following it with reports on the situation for their own readers or listeners. *Interest* magazine, associated with the same fellowship of churches (so-called Plymouth Brethren) as Emmaus, published a very positive article asking for prayer and financial support from around the world.

WVCY, a television station in Michigan, did a docudrama using actual voices from the taped interviews with the police and illustrating my perspective on how the police had mishandled the case and lied to me. A television station in downstate

Illinois also covered the story, with Lois's participation. Herman Bailey's "Action 60s" TV show flew Lois to Florida as part of its coverage of our plight.

One glaring exception to the factual, positive coverage was a report that appeared in *Moody Monthly* magazine in October of 1983, a report substantially in error. Over the years Moody Radio Network ran a number of reports based on rumor, despite our efforts to keep them informed of the facts. On one occasion, after I'd been released, Moody announced to its national radio audience that I had been returned to prison after the discovery of conclusive evidence linking me to the crime. I heard the report from my home and wondered if Moody knew something I didn't.

I have no explanation for this negative coverage, but I know that I felt betrayed by it, since I regarded myself as being in the same "camp." Even when my attorneys offered Moody documents to refute their "facts," they declined, and they have never apologized to me.

For the most part, however, the publicity, to the extent that it was factual, was favorable to our cause. After the WVCY docudrama, the *Wednesday Journal,* a widely distributed free newspaper in the near-west Chicago suburbs, came out with a favorable story. Editor Dan Haley wrote that the film, along with the tapes on which it was based, raised doubts about my case. The article detailed how I had been deceived and bullied by the police in their efforts to secure a confession.

A physics professor at Eastern Illinois University mounted a letter-writing campaign on my behalf. He and Pastor Goss put together a fact sheet along with press clippings, sending out packages to virtually all news sources with more than fifty thousand readers or viewers. The Chicago affiliate of NBC became interested largely through the efforts of newscaster Debra

Norville, a Christian who went on to host "The Today Show" for a time. The story ran as a two-parter on the 10 o'clock news, and it effectively raised doubts about my conviction.

Over the months we received mountains of letters, many of them containing money. Lois cared about all the letters, but she also had to care for the children. She simply could not keep up with it all. On occasion she'd have a woman from the church over to help open the mail. One day the checks we received came to over $2,000 (only a fraction of our legal fees). Nevertheless, we could not believe that our lives had become that important to so many people. This was yet another sign of God's faithfulness.

Lois and I needed all the support we could get as the legal system dragged on and on. Tom Decker had formally filed an appeal in June of 1983, a year after the trial. We'd been told that it would take six months to a year from the time the appeal was filed before we'd receive word from the appellate court on the status of our appeal. The court usually announced on Wednesdays which, if any, decisions were forthcoming on Friday. So after a year was up, we began living each week in anticipation of Wednesday. But when a couple of months worth of Wednesdays passed with no sign of any movement in our case, we quit torturing ourselves with unfounded expectations.

We waited in constant expectation of God's deliverance through a miracle. At times I wondered if I might have to serve the whole sentence. But part of me could not believe that. We felt that God must be doing something we could not discern. Whatever His purposes were, they lay outside our normal ways of interpreting God's actions. There were no easy answers. God would not be placed in a box.

Services at the prison chapel sometimes made things worse, as they provided occasions to meditate on my pain and frustration. What's more, most of the chaplains' perspective on Scripture was such that I sometimes wondered if we believed in the same God, even though some of their teachings broadened my understanding in certain areas. In any case, I kept going to chapel, partly because I felt a responsibility to other believers who were struggling with their own issues in their own ways. We found encouragement from one another.

As I'd done all along, during this time I tried to be aware of God's purposes. I'd learned of the healing power of forgiveness. And I believed God was honoring my ministry as editor of the prison newspaper. But I constantly tried to look for additional ways He might be calling me to grow.

At one point I was reminded again of what I was like prior to this experience. Lois and I had made a trip to Maine to minister with Lois's brother and his wife in a local church. Lois's sister-in-law suggested to Lois that God was allowing all this "to break Steve." Her lack of empathy made me think about how we must have come across during those trips to Maine. Perhaps I was not so much ministering among the people as I was preaching at them. God was continuing to humble me.

The most important lesson during this time, however, came from a totally different direction. Through Joe Ritchie, who became a friend and a counselor, God urged me not to lower my view of self but to raise it. I would come to believe that outward signs of arrogance are sometimes signs of inner insecurity. Perhaps my efforts to succeed at ministry were rooted in the feeling that I was not good enough in God's sight, that despite being saved I had to somehow earn God's love and prove to Him my faithfulness. I would deny verbally to anyone my belief that I had to "earn" anything. I knew the right language; but like many, I was fearful of God.

As the legal bills piled up, Joe stepped in to help. His futures trading company had begun to enjoy huge successes in the stock exchange. More importantly, I cannot put a monetary value on the spiritual guidance he provided.

Joe never once pitied me. He wanted me to view what I was going through not as a problem but as an opportunity. He urged me to recognize and affirm God's goodness and to understand all the implications of my identity as a saint. This was a new concept to me. Its reality would take time to sink in.

This process entailed being honest with others and with God about Lois's and my true feelings. Joe did not use the same trite phrases used by others to encourage us. Nor did he let me get away with them. He knew that the process of sorting through our feelings and of understanding God as completely as possible could be accomplished only through brutal honesty. It entailed holding longtime beliefs up against the light of Scripture and reality.

I was incredulous that Joe invited me to call him at his home or at his office. Sometimes we'd talk for an hour while he ignored the phones ringing behind him. Once I told him I was doing okay, and he sensed my insincerity. He knew that I, like countless other believers, was saying that because I felt it was expected of me. I did not know at the time that there was nothing wrong about admitting I was hurting.

"No," said Joe one time, after I told him that all was well, "how are you really?" I paused for a moment and then from somewhere deep inside replied, "I hurt." Joe then went on to tell me about a time in his life when he could not hurt outwardly because of how he felt God would react. Although it was an extremely painful period, Joe told me, at the time he believed Christians should always have "the joy of the Lord."

This was the first step. I would have other conversations with Joe during which I would gradually be able to acknowledge that I was angry at God, disappointed with Him, that I wanted to know why He was putting me through this.

Joe encouraged me to believe that there is no growth without honesty and that the God in whom I believed was big enough to take whatever I had to say to Him that was based on honesty and sincerity. Even so, I felt guilty about questioning God in this way. Most, if not all, of my Christian friends, I believed, would not accept this kind of attitude toward God.

I then offered to Joe a brief theology of myself, explaining that I was positionally righteous because Christ had chosen me to be saved. But ultimately I was a sinner, a worm in a King's clothes, undeserving of anything good, unworthy to question God even in the smallest way. Though I believed I was saved by grace, my true identity was that of a sinner.

Joe listened patiently. Then he responded with one, undeniable truth. "Steve," he said, "God is good."

I am convinced that believers, in general, do not comprehend the profound implications of the simple statement, "God is good." In his book Why? theologian A. van de Beek points out that throughout the ages, people's concept of God as all-powerful was a given. Nobody questioned that. To be all-powerful was built into the definition of God. Whether or not God has to be good, however, is another matter.

"God is good," said Joe. And, of course, I thought I believed that. At some level at least I could affirm that God cared for me more than I could imagine, that His goodness included a love for me that had no limits. Would a God who is that loving and that good reject me merely for expressing to Him my deepest, most important feelings?

The light of understanding was beginning to break through the darkness of my insecurity and confusion. Yes, I had sinned, many times. I knew it, and God knew it. But did God want me to think of myself as a sinner? Joe urged me to consider otherwise. After all, I had been born again. My true, deepest identity was as one born of the seed of Jesus Christ. I was a child of the King. Now the full implications of that reality were starting to sink in. Life-changing truth was helping me step into the light of my true identity as a beliver.

"Too many Christians have bought into guilty living," Joe continued, "because they haven't realized who they are. Someone who truly believes God is good, who is born of Him, should not live in fear of being honest with God."

I slept more soundly that night than I'd slept in a year. The joy in my heart was comparable to the joy of salvation. I was not a worm. I was God's child. I was a friend of Jesus Christ, a brother. Had I grown up with Him in Israel, we would have played together. Someday we will be in Heaven together. Though I might sin, that sin does not reflect my true identity.

The joy was still with me in the morning. The blinders were off. I felt more alive. The peace that came with this fuller realization of my true identity was greater than any prison experience could suppress.

11

A Question with No Answer

The amount of real trust we have in God is sometimes best measured by the depth of the doubt and the seriousness of the questions with which we are willing to live.

Robert J. Wicks

ON ALMOST EVERY visit to the prison between November of 1984 to July of 1985, my son Paul, now five, at the end of the visit would beg me to come home. Once, after a prison picnic, he cried so hard I returned to him after walking away. I held him tightly, trying to calm him down.

At the main gate he began crying again. A woman guard asked him what he was crying about. "Because I don't want to leave my daddy here," was his reply. No words can express the heaviness of my heart in that moment of seeing my son in such pain, but knowing there was nothing I could do.

One day in May I spoke with Paul on the phone. He told me he'd been crying a lot lately. This five-year-old and his dad proceeded to have a heart-to-heart talk. He had some difficult questions for me: Will the guards let you come home if you ask them? Why not? Will the judges let you come home if we ask them? Will God let you come home if we ask Him? Little did he know how many times I had asked God that very question.

Before hanging up the phone, we prayed together, petitioning God to release me. "Did God hear our prayer?" he asked. "Is He going to let you come home?"

Paul's questions poured forth from a pure heart. It was important for me to hear his honesty, even though some of his questions I could not answer, and the answers I could offer he would not understand.

His efforts, however, spurred me to consider how I should approach my Heavenly Father. Would He feel any different about my honest pleadings than I felt toward my son? For the next three months I cried out to God. Virtually every day, once every two or three hours, I called on Him to deliver me. I had no expectations, nor would I think any less of Him if my cries went unheeded, for I knew that my Father was good and that there were things I did not understand. But it was important for me to express to Him honestly how I felt.

Based on my confidence in God's goodness, I no longer had any reservations about asking Him the once forbidden question, Why? His shoulders, I was convinced, were big enough to handle my questions and fears. After all, God knows all about fear, about the pain of separation and of loss. He understands the need for answers to His children's deepest questions. And my question came out of a wonderful sense of relationship.

No longer did I believe that He would rebuke my expressions of honesty. Instead, I believed even more than before that if He would not grant my requests, He would provide comfort, that He would reassure me through His Word or thorough the Holy Spirit. Just as a loving earthly father would not resent or rebuff the pleadings, the painful questions, of his beloved child, neither would God, who loves His children more deeply than any human father can ever love.

In the bowels of that concrete-and-steel jungle, I came to believe that to ask why is more a profession of faith in a God who is loving and good than it is an expression of doubt. No longer did I fear losing God's favor, and no longer would I condemn myself for expressing my pain to my Father as my son had expressed his pain to me.

As van de Beek writes, it is only in the context of the security of the Father's love that we ask Him about his "management." And we ask Him "because He is most important to us, because we cannot ignore Him, because it is impossible for us to be indifferent to Him, and we cannot be content not to know Him. At the same time, however, we know that we only dare ask these questions in the knowledge that, essentially, we already know Him as the one who loves us and *knows* us. If we want to fight through the question of 'why?' to the very bottom, the way is that of the child, not of the proud titan."

Specifically, my biggest "why" was, "Why does nothing ever seem to happen in my case?" The unexpected waiting prior to the trial was difficult, but at least then I was on the outside, with my family. The dull routine of prison life was bearable largely because the end seemed in sight almost from the beginning. But now I wondered if the end would ever be in sight.

We'd thought it would take six months to a year for a decision on the appeal. But almost three years passed, and there was no sign of any movement.

Despite everything I'd learned about myself and my relationship with God, and despite my ultimate confidence in His goodness and love, life was a daily, monotonous grind. It took its toll on Lois and me. Maybe Thomas à Kempis or Madame

Guyon, a godly, devout woman of a past century, would have handled it better. But we were who we were, and we were doing the best we could.

Usually if I was down, Lois was there to pick me up. Or vice versa. But I recall one phone call when we both were depressed and frustrated, each of us hurting too much to reach out to the other. We blew up at one another on the phone. For a time it seemed it was better if we did not talk to each other so much.

So uncertain was I about the appeal ever being heard that I enrolled in a Moody Bible Institute correspondence course in Greek for May, June, and July. Despite my bad experience with Moody, I regarded the correspondence school and the media division as two different entities. And I'd heard nothing but good things about the correspondence program.

We also published all the legal briefs in the case for interested readers and made plans to participate in another television documentary.

On July 27, 1985, Lois and I got bad news about a friend for whom we'd been praying. His cancer had taken a turn for the worse; he was given only a short time to live. On that same day, however—after three years of waiting—we learned that the appellate court had finally reached a decision and would release it the following Friday.

Earlier in the week the Illinois Supreme Court had decided that, because of the inactivity in the case, it would consider granting bond. We did not know if the appellate court's decision to publish now was coincidental, or if it might be a negative sign, a move to ensure that I would not be released any time soon.

We waited tensely. Days spent in prison are long enough, but those next few days seemed even longer. I had arranged to call Lois at noon on Friday to get the news. But at 11:30 A.M. I received word that a visitor was waiting to see me. I knew it had to be Lois, but I did not know what to make of it.

If there was no news—another false alarm—she would not have come to visit. I prayed briefly and tried to think. Why would Lois come out instead of keeping the phone appointment? Would she visit to tell me bad news or good news?

I went to the housing unit to check out for the visit and to change clothes. I stripped completely naked, and the symbolism was not lost upon me. Once more I realized that I was ultimately naked—vulnerable and helpless—before God. But I knew that was a good thing, not something to fear. "Which is it?" I prayed, even though I believed I knew.

I began to think it must be good news. So many times Lois had given me bad news over the phone; surely she would have simply kept that pattern if the news were bad. But after all we'd been through, she would not want to miss the opportunity to be there personally as a messenger of good news.

Hurriedly I dressed and rushed off to the visiting room. The moment I walked through the door, Lois grabbed me and began dancing with me, pulling me around the room while shouting, "A complete reversal! A complete reversal!"

I was jubilant but confused. "No," I said. "You mean a reversal and remand for a new trial." (By then we were fairly proficient at legalese.) To my shock, Lois corrected me. It was indeed an outright reversal.

The most we had ever hoped for was to be granted a new trial. The appellate court went beyond that, overturning my guilty verdict based on insufficient evidence. Everything we'd been saying all along had finally been heard and believed. I was delirious. Freedom, it seemed, was just around the corner, a matter of going through the formal release procedures.

When the people at the doctor's office where Lois worked

heard the news, they were jubilant. All of her coworkers loved Lois deeply. They had followed the case for years, upholding us regularly in their prayers. Abandoning the typical office decorum, the secretaries let fly all manner of papers into the air as they shouted with joy. Sharing our sorrow had prepared them to share in our happiness. They exemplified people in various parts of the country and the world who rejoiced after having struggled with us for so long.

Those next few days were filled with new plans and fresh hopes. Though it seemed that everything we'd hoped and prayed for had finally come to pass, however, we would soon learn that our celebrating was premature. The only flaw in the appellate court's decision, from our perspective, was that it was not unanimous. Of the three appellate court judges, one had issued a dissenting vote, upholding the original verdict. The dissent perhaps gave more credence to the state's impending appeal of the reversal.

The state had two weeks to file its appeal with the Illinois Supreme Court. That happened, as we expected. The bail set by the appellate court allowed for my release on my signature alone. The state filed a motion to vacate that order. On August 15, my release was stayed pending a decision on these matters by the Illinois Supreme Court.

We hoped, as always, that the decision would come shortly. But on September 12, five weeks after the appellate court's reversal, we were still waiting. I counted the days since I'd set foot outside a prison: 1,231. We had a good visit with Lois's parents, who came in from Maine after hearing the good news. The press, of course, was all over us for interviews.

Joe had bought us a new car, a minivan, to be delivered upon my release. It was gathering dust. A wreath of flowers Lois had bought to celebrate my return home wilted in the refrigerator.

(She'd actually bought it even prior to the appellate court's reversal, as a statement of faith.) The waiting continued.

Then on October 3, the Illinois Supreme Court published and mailed its decision. The news was not good. It decided to hear my case. Agreeing with state prosecutors, the court deemed that bond should be revoked and my release stayed until the state's appeal was heard. Word reached our attorneys on October 4, five years to the day since the crime was committed.

We were crushed. To have our hopes dashed in this way was the ultimate cruelty. It had taken three years for our first appeal to be heard. Would it take another three years of incarceration before the next appeal was decided upon?

When Lois came in for a visit, we held hands tightly, trying to support one another. On top of all we had been through, this was something we just could not accept. Our victory celebration had once more been transformed into defeat. It seemed to us a cruel cosmic joke of the highest degree. Was there any justice left in the universe? we wondered.

Three years earlier, living with similar news over the course of a few weeks had almost robbed me of my sanity. Now here we were again, with three and a half years gone by and nothing changed. Lois and I simply had no tears left to cry. It was as if we'd used them all up. And so we sat and laughed at this joke. Even though we hurt, we laughed. Inside, however, we were crying. And in our pain we hoped for a time when our laughter would be genuine again.

12

A Family Reunion

And if we know that He hears us, whatever we ask, we know that we have the petitions that we have asked of Him.

1 John 5:15, NKJV

AFTER LOIS LEFT, I returned to my cell and fell asleep for two hours. I awoke with a headache, the bad news still hovering over me like a cloud. I recalled months earlier having read an article on a decision rendered by the Illinois Supreme Court. As an aside in its written ruling, the court had stated, "We decide what happens in Illinois." This struck me as the height of arrogance.

Lying in my cell with my eyes fixed on the ceiling, I spoke to the Lord from my heart: "God, You are our Supreme Court. You are the One to whom we are appealing to overrule arrogant men." I mulled over the thought of at least another full year in prison. I confessed to my Father, "Lord, You know how I feel.

You know where I've been. You must know that I cannot do another year in prison."

Searching for comfort, I opened my Bible and began to read. I'd been reading through the entire Bible and had just arrived at the Gospels. Starting with the sixth chapter of Matthew, certain passages, and in particular all the miracles Christ had performed, began to grab my attention. And something unusual began to take place as I read.

In the past, even in times when my faith in God was strong, I had little or no expectation of God's supernatural intervention getting me out of the mess I was in any time soon. God had granted me the grace to accept my fate. But as far as expecting God to deliver me was concerned, my faith had gone stale.

Now, however, something different was happening. My trust in God began to warm and glow within me. My headache faded, and the darkness of my spirit began to dissipate. As I read about miracles that had taken place long ago, I had the strongest impression that they could and were happening today.

Certain phrases leapt out from the pages of the King James Bible:

Matthew 6:33-34: "Seek ye first the kingdom of God, and his righteousness. Take therefore no thought for the morrow: for the morrow shall take thought for the things of itself. Sufficient unto the day is the evil thereof." I began to block out all thoughts of the storm that raged around us.

7:1: "Judge not, that ye be not judged." I determined to leave the judgment of my earthly judges to God and to expel all anger and vengeful thinking.

7:7-9: "Ask, and it shall be given you . . . what man is there of you, whom if his son ask bread, will he give him a stone?" This renewed my confidence in my Father's wisdom and love.

7:29: "For [Jesus] taught them as one having authority, and

not as the scribes." I affirmed afresh that God had the final authority. My hope was gone. Lois's was gone. Joe's was gone. There was nothing left for our attorneys to do. But God was bigger than any of us could figure.

Chapters 8 and 9 of Matthew once more took me through Jesus' miracles. He calmed a troubled sea, cast out demons, healed the sick and crippled, and opened the eyes of the blind. God began to impress on me that I should pray for a miracle of my own.

After doing just that, I continued to read and pray over the miracles in Matthew. I called Lois five times that evening to encourage her with Scripture. The first time she wept bitterly. But her spirits picked up as the evening went on. She sensed my excitement. We both knew I could be wrong, and if that was the case I was acting very odd. But we knew also that I could be right in believing that our miracle was just around the corner.

The next day Lois called her mother to tell her the bad news. A normal response from her would have been to advise us to accept this and to continue to trust the Lord for grace and strength. But on this particular day she told Lois not to accept the court's ruling as final. She urged us instead to believe that God could do something wonderful.

This unprompted response of faith and expectation, coupled with my confidence, got Lois's attention. It confirmed to her that something out of the ordinary could be happening here. "If my mother says that," Lois remarked to me, "it's already a miracle."

I asked Lois if she'd called Joe yet. I knew he would be worried about us, and I wanted him to know that we were okay and that he should not be discouraged.

"I've tried," she said, "but he doesn't answer." Joe was indeed discouraged. He was afraid we might call, and he was not sure he could face us. He loved us deeply. So many times he had encouraged us to open our minds and hearts to a new understanding of ourselves and our relationship with God. He helped us come to grips with the full reality of a loving God, a God who sometimes allows His children to experience pain in order to draw them closer.

Now Joe was experiencing some of that pain. It hurt us to think that he was hurting. The teacher had become the student. We finally got a message through to Joe that our spirits were high, our faith was strong, and our expectations for a miracle were great.

I fasted for three days. Unknown at the time to me, three Christian friends in the prison—independently of one another—had also begun fasting and praying on my behalf, even though they were unaware of the recent developments. Bobby, a black brother from Chicago, fasted for seven days, going from a large, muscular man to bones. Two other friends fasted for shorter periods of time over the span of two weeks.

Lois began to pray urgently for a miracle. Knowing how much we both enjoyed the beauty of autumn, she prayed specifically that God would allow me to leave prison in time to enjoy the colors of fall.

She picked out one particular tree, designating it as a sort of barometer of God's faithfulness. She convinced herself that before that tree was in full splendor, I would be released.

Believing that God would answer that prayer, she marked the tree's progress each day she drove by. First a few leaves started changing, then a few more. When it reached its point of full beauty, Lois prayed, "Let this be the day."

But soon all the leaves were brown and beginning to fall. Each day she noticed fewer and fewer leaves on the tree. Finally, one day in late October the tree was totally bare.

It was hard for her to be too disappointed, however, because my confidence remained undaunted. God continued to speak to me about a miracle. I felt certain it would take place before the month of October was out.

One day after a visit, Lois and the children discovered another kind of tree, an unusual pine tree whose large branches dipped downward, in a little park in Centralia. It was the kind with the branches low enough for kids to climb. The children got underneath and climbed up inside, disappearing as Lois watched from a distance. As they played in the tree, Lois realized that she'd never even noticed this tree before, despite its size. Its consistent green beauty had been overshadowed by all the colors.

In those moments God granted Lois a measure of comfort and hope. No matter when I was released, she realized, God would provide beauty. The colorful trees were indeed beautiful. But their time had come and gone. God's beauty was more like the evergreen—constant, steady, and strong.

Scriptures relevant to my situation continued to impress me with special meaning. Matthew 10:39: "He that loseth his life for my sake shall find it." These days, it was God's glory alone that I sought. There was nothing of my own self-seeking left. I realized that, outside of God, my life had no meaning. And yet, as a believer, I could be confident that I was never outside of God. I felt that this was in some sense the climax of all I was meant to learn. Lois and I were in the midst of an intense experience of God's reality and love. Both of us were believing fully that He would provide a miracle. On one visit Lois said to me, "It's as if we have inside information." We prayed with ease for something we fully believed was His will, though it seemed almost impossible.

Matthew 15:21-28 tells the story of a woman, an outsider

from Canaan, in search of her daughter's deliverance from a demon. Jesus seemed tentative, claiming that He had been sent "unto the lost sheep of the house of Israel." But when she pointed out her willingness to accept the crumbs from the Master's table, He rewarded her faith, restoring her daughter to wholeness. Like that woman nearly two thousand years ago, we believed in a God so great and awesome that the mere crumbs of His power would be enough.

I read Matthew 17, which speaks of a faith that can move mountains, believing that this powerful faith was active in my life at this time. Foolhardy or not, I simply had no room for any doubt that God would perform a miracle soon.

Late in October I was interviewed by a Christian radio station in Nevada, which was doing an update. I shared with the audience the latest news on the court front. But I also went out on a limb, proclaiming that God had been speaking to our hearts with regard to an October miracle.

I was being recruited for prison events scheduled for November. I wanted to tell people that I didn't expect to be in prison by then, but I did not want rumors to spread that I was considering an attempt to break out. (Such rumors had made the rounds previously.)

In mid-October my lawyers had filed a routine request for bond, then became engrossed in work on other cases. On October 31, Halloween Day, I awoke and prayed. This was the final day of what I believed was a deadline for the miracle for which I and others had been praying. I didn't know what would happen or how, but I believed something would.

I showered, shaved, and dressed as usual. I drank my coffee with joy in my heart, feeling strong. I'd arranged to call Lois at noon, but she called prior to that and left a message for me to call her.

When I did, she told me the details of the miracle we'd been expecting. The high court had met in a closed session and issued an order for bond in the amount of $45,000—the same amount that had been set upon my arrest. Lois said that one of our attorneys had trembled with excitement on the phone as he shared this good news. He had given the bond request virtually no chance for success. We may never know why the court decided as it did.

We found this out on a Thursday. Joe felt electrified by the news, as did all of our supporters. He immediately made arrangements to provide the bond money. Normally the process of being released takes a few days, as it must run through the state capitol to court officials and finally to the prison. But Joe was determined to pull it off in time for me to be home by the weekend. Documents were mailed overnight from Springfield, and Joe hustled them around Chicago. Then on Friday afternoon, November 1, he, along with a small entourage that included Tom Decker, hopped on Joe's plane and flew to Centralia despite high winds and lightning.

Soon, after three and a half grueling years behind steel and concrete, I would walk out of prison a free man. All those times when the facts and legal arguments all seemed to be on our side, God had remained silent. Even when the appellate court nullified the original guilty verdict, the state found a way to keep me in jail, and God did not intervene. But now, when we were powerless, out of options, and with almost nothing to hope for, He made his presence known in a mighty way.

It was as if God was saying to me, "If you think you can ever even begin to figure Me out, to determine how I should act or what I must do, you do not know Me. Even your greatest possible efforts to understand My ways amount to nothing. No matter how good things may look for you, I might delay deliverance for reasons you do not understand. But when things look bad for you, when your hope has run dry, when your situation seems impossible, I can break through. There is no problem I cannot solve, no pain I cannot ease."

Most importantly, I believe God wanted me to know that He loved me more than I could imagine, more than I could believe. Even through the times of anger and doubt, He continued to love me. The reality of God's sovereignty was impressed upon me in a mighty, unforgettable way.

❦

In some ways I preferred to spend one final weekend at Centralia. I wanted time to sort through my thoughts, to tie up some loose ends. From the beginning everything had happened so slowly, had dragged out for so long. Now, when the moment finally arrived, I wanted things to slow down. I felt a little like a kid who got straight to Christmas day without fully experiencing the excitement of anticipation.

On the other hand, there is no bad time to leave prison. And I knew that my friends and family wanted me out as soon as possible.

Lois and a few friends picked up Joe, Tom, and the others at the airport and drove them to the prison. They'd made the flight despite near zero visibility. Lois told the kids something about a special visit to the prison to see Daddy. They were used to going on a weekday morning or afternoon. She didn't want them to tell them I would be coming home, because no one knew if the paperwork would be done in time.

In a magnanimous gesture, the warden at Centralia, after finding out that the papers were being flown down, authorized overtime for his staff. Nevertheless, no one could be sure I would get out that night until I walked through the last set of prison doors.

Later Lois would tell me the story of how everyone waited excitedly in the yard outside the prison gates. The children began to suspect something was up. One of Paul's five-year-old buddies told him that his dad was coming home from jail tonight, but Paul refused to believe it. Each argued his case, as children do, and Katherine picked up on it. She approached Joe and asked him, "Is my daddy coming home today?"

Joe answered with the question, "Would you like him to come home today?" When Katherine said yes, Joe gave her a confident wink.

Finally Lois saw me inside, walking alone toward the exit, carrying a small bag of personal items. I had four sets of doors to go through, then three, then two, and then one. Then I saw for the first time the prison entrance that Lois had come through so many times. As I stepped once more into freedom, strangely I felt little emotion. All the highs and lows were gone. For what seemed like several minutes, everyone just stared at me, as if observing a miracle.

Little Vicki broke away from the pack and wrapped herself around my legs. A second or two later Lois pushed forward, crushing my neck with her embrace and crying uncontrollably. The only other tears came from a prison guard, who stood nearby weeping. He said he was a Christian, but up until then the nature of his job prevented him from getting too personal with me. Now things were different. He said he'd been praying for me and that he was glad he was scheduled to work that day so he could see this happen.

This was a time for laughter and unbridled joy. Hugs, smiles, and kisses flew in all directions. My ordeal was far from over, and

I knew that. Though I did not know the details, I knew we had plenty of pain left to endure, many more tears to come. But not tonight.

I've heard Super Bowl and World Series winners say they can't describe their good feeling. I suppose I can't fully describe the joy I felt upon being released. I was free again, reunited with those I cared about most.

13

"You Excel Them All"

Strength and honor are her clothing; she shall rejoice in time to come. . . . She watches over the ways of her household, and does not eat the bread of idleness.

Proverbs 31:25, 27, NKJV, on the capable wife

COUPLE OF WEEKS after my release, we invited our friends and supporters to a celebration at Woodside Bible Chapel in suburban Chicago. We wanted to glorify God and declare victory over the powers of evil.

What I wanted most to do that evening, however, was to pay a long overdue tribute to Lois. I had determined while in prison to present her with a plaque at my first public appearance following my release.

I kissed her in front of God and everyone else as I handed her the plaque, which came as a total surprise to her. It was the highlight of my evening. Part of the inscription came from Proverbs 31: "Many daughters have done virtuously, but thou excellest them all."

Another part of the inscription read:

To Lois, from Steve:

In commemoration—and with deep love and devotion—for your five years of love and faithfulness while in the midst of the fiery trial of our faith.

I shudder when I reflect upon what my prison experience would have been like without her. It's possible I would not have survived, since she and the children represented at least some earthly purpose for me to live.

Never wavering in her devotion, Lois visited the prison as often as she could, and she was always there when I called. She told me all the stories surrounding the children, trying to involve me in the life of the family. Perhaps most importantly, she comforted me with evidence of God's faithfulness in her life.

During my incarceration, I was fully aware that many, if not most, wives in Lois's position left their husbands altogether—not over the issue of guilt or innocence, but based on the practical considerations of what was best for the rest of the family.

Lois had offers to take extended vacations far away from Illinois in order to relieve the pressure. She declined them all. When I was transferred downstate to Centralia, some of our friends and relatives advised her to remain in the Chicago area, where she and the children already had a network of support. This advice went unheeded.

Lois truly believed that life would be more bearable for her and for the children if they were as close as possible to me. She chose to endure more than what she had to endure. As mentioned previously, one way she did this was to live, essentially, out of boxes the whole time I was imprisoned. Through this she affirmed that the injustice was only temporary. She committed herself to experiencing each of my disappointments as her own.

Lois based all her decisions not only on what was practical, nor on what would make life more bearable for her and the children, but also on principle. She has such a staunchness about her convictions that when she believes something is right, it's almost impossible to convince her otherwise.

In this case she believed it was right to display her commitment by remaining as close to me as possible. After all, she reasoned, she had made a vow, a promise of loyalty to me that encompassed times of prosperity and poverty, health and sickness, good times and bad. To Lois, that vow also included times of freedom and incarceration. Lois's devotion, of course, was attributable largely to the fact that she had no doubts about my innocence. Nevertheless, people would marvel at her example of loyalty. Lois, however, genuinely could not understand how anyone could think that what she was doing was unusual or heroic in any way. She wondered how anyone who had taken marriage vows could possible do anything different.

This rock-solid commitment was both a cause and an effect of Lois's toughness as a person, one of the most strong-willed people I've ever known. At many times during this ordeal, words of advice and encouragement for Lois became as irrelevant as a raindrop on the ocean. There were no answers, no shortcuts on the path of pain she had chosen. She simply had to gut it out, pure and simple. Lois's father, who has eight other children, some of whom are missionaries and Christian leaders, told me once that none of them could have endured this experience like Lois did.

Any single mother of three small children knows just how hard life was for Lois while I was in prison. Add to that her part-time job, the time and energy associated with her commitment to being a faithful wife, and her efforts to respond to the hundreds of letters and phone calls she received each year about the case, and the word *stressful* falls far short. Many would conclude that her life was impossible. The hardest times for Lois came in the evenings after putting the children to bed. It was then when she realized most that where there ought to be two of us, there was only one.

Sometimes I would call at 8:30 at night (this was late for Lois) just to talk, and she would fall asleep. Though at first this would annoy me, upon later reflection I'd realize that life for her was no picnic. The fact that she could fall asleep on the phone revealed to me that she was driving herself to her very limits.

Often the expressions of concern on our behalf were awkward, requiring that Lois develop the additional skill of diplomacy. Through it all she had to be both strong and soft. Once every month or so Lois granted herself the luxury of a good cry, just to vent all the emotional pain and stress. When she would start crying, she could not stop for hours. It was a survival technique, one she would like to have employed more frequently. But the experience would wipe her out for half a day, and that was a luxury she could not afford very often.

But if this experience made Lois a tougher person, it also made her more compassionate. She will never, for example, have quite the same view of people who are on welfare. How vividly she recalls the experience of being on public aid throughout most of the time I was in prison.

Lois regards her experience of using food stamps as being among the most humiliating things she's ever had to endure. For most people a trip to the grocery store is a routine part of life. Some find it relaxing, even enjoyable. But for Lois during those years, every food shopping trip was an occasion for emotional trauma.

She felt that people in the checkout line were watching her and judging her; indeed, many were. She never felt free to get any candy or soda for the children. On one occasion she put some steaks into the grocery cart and prepared a defense for anyone who might challenge her. She would explain that she was not planning on serving them straight, but on cutting them up as part of meals of Chinese food.

Sure enough, when she got to the checkout line, the cashier called attention to the steaks, asking what someone on public aid was doing taking home such a luxury item. Lois immediately launched into her justification. But when she got out to the car, she felt both hurt and angry that she owed anyone any explanations. From that point on, she chose longer lines just to avoid the same cashier.

Being on food stamps required that Lois fill out the same forms month after month and visit government offices for interviews verifying the needs of the family. She now understands how people caught up in that system can become callous, even angry and belligerent. Saying, "I don't care what others think" is a coping mechanism, a way of dealing with the dehumanizing embarrassment caused by the system. Lois still recalls the feeling of freedom she had the first time she went through a grocery line again with cash.

Several years later in Springfield, long after I'd been released, Lois found herself in line behind a young woman with food stamps. The woman took them out of her purse and tried to hide them, just as Lois used to do. She was also trying to manage a young child, who was kicking a little and crying a lot.

Lois admits there was a time when she would have leaned toward viewing this woman as a charity case, as just another unwed mother living off the system. But on this day she looked at the woman ahead of her and saw herself.

Cashiers generally don't like food stamps, because they can slow them down. On this particular day the store was crowded, and Lois could tell that the presumably middle-class people in line behind her were growing impatient. She could also tell by the expression on the woman's face that this experience was torture for her.

At that moment, more than anything else in the world, Lois wanted to help that woman, to ease her embarrassment even a little bit, to let her know that at least one person in that line was in her corner. But Lois knew there was nothing she could do. To offer the woman money or to comment on her difficulties would be to call more attention to her situation. Lois knew from personal experience that what the woman really wanted was simply to disappear. There in a grocery store line tears began to well up in Lois's eyes; a lump came to her throat.

Things got worse for the woman when her child kicked the food stamps out of her hands and all over the floor. At that point Lois intervened and asked if she could hold the child for a few moments. The woman allowed Lois to help and thanked her. But Lois was every bit as thankful for this opportunity to express what she was feeling.

My prison experience also presented Lois with the challenge of seeking God. Through this time she learned to recognize and even to anticipate what she regarded as clear signs of God's faithfulness.

Although Lois rarely watched television, one night she and the children gathered around the set to view the movie *Chariots of Fire*. At age four, Paul could understand only the most rudimentary elements of the plot, but he knew it concerned a young man who was in a race.

The next day, according to Lois, Paul got out of bed and came out to the kitchen. As he rubbed his bleary eyes, the first words out of his mouth were, "Mommy, Daddy's comin' out a winner. Daddy's comin' out a winner." Lois chose to view that incident as God speaking to her through our son.

Lois told me of another occasion, Easter Sunday in fact, when she was trying to get to church early so she could sing in a cantata. She looked in all the normal places but could not find the keys to the car.

As she tore up the apartment looking for them, she expressed her frustration aloud to God, hollering things like, "Why won't You help me find those keys? I'm going to church, aren't I?"

Then she figured she'd try a different strategy since they were running late. She said a quick prayer to God, apologizing for her attitude. Immediately after the prayer was over she ransacked the house again but still could not find the keys.

By this time they were hopelessly late not just for choir, but for church. The realization began to come over Lois that God was more concerned about the example she was setting for the children than about whether she made it to church on time or at all. She knew her attitude had been wrong, and she confessed as much to the children and apologized to them. Now, truly humbled, she sat on the bed and prayed to God, asking Him to give her the grace to put things in proper perspective. The moment she opened her eyes, she saw the keys lying right on the floor in front of her.

For me, however, the story that stands out the most is the one surrounding the children's (especially Paul's) longing for a pet dog. One evening Paul was crying about it, and Lois simply had to explain to him that the rules at the apartment complex where they lived did not allow animals. The best Lois could do was to tell Paul to pray to God about wanting a dog. Inside she agonized.

The next morning Lois looked outside, and there was Paul playing with a big, shaggy white dog similar to Barkley on "Sesame Street." Soon the other children joined him, and they had a wonderful time. But they were frustrated and sad when they had to bid the dog farewell because they had errands to run.

As soon as Lois and the kids got on the road, they spotted in the car in front of them a big boxer dog with his head hanging out the window. This guy's jowls were flapping in the wind; saliva was flying everywhere. The children acted like it was the funniest thing they'd ever seen as they rolled in their seats with laughter.

After a while, however, Lois had to turn off to go in a different direction. But before the kids could catch their breath, sure enough, they'd gotten in behind yet another car with a dog inside. This one was a small dog, a bouncer who was putting on a show, going up and down, appearing and disappearing, again to the children's absolute delight. The memory of that delight lingered for quite a while.

The shaggy white dog never showed up again, and Lois does not recall ever seeing a dog in another car in that neighborhood. Admittedly, this is not enough "evidence" to convince a skeptic of God's existence. But Lois and I were not and are not skeptics. We saw in the seemingly common, everyday events of that morning God's answer to a small boy's prayer for a dog.

❦

Throughout the final year of my incarceration, Lois experienced God's faithfulness virtually every morning. In the quiet moments before the hectic pace of the day would begin, Lois spent time in prayer, Scripture reading, and meditation. Through providing the comfort, security, and assurance Lois experienced during those times, God became a husband to her in my absence.

Among Lois's most precious memories of feeling near to God are those mornings she spent alone with Him. Sometimes she would have only a few minutes and so would ask God to come quickly to her. And He always did, giving her some special insight or providing the spiritual strength she needed to face another day.

To this day, Lois has not experienced the presence of the living God like she did during that time. She even misses it. It was never quite the same after my release. She believes that was God's way of telling her that it was time to return to me.

Lois does not believe that God is ever far from any of His people. She does believe that God abides in a special way with those who are widows or are alone for some other reason. She freely shares with these people her testimony, telling them that God would not say He would be their husband if He didn't mean it, encouraging them to seek the comfort and strength that is available to them through the living Lord.

Indeed, many daughters have done well, Lois Linscott, but you excel them all.

14

Learning to Be a Family Again

God is at work in all the kaleidoscoping family transitions: not only in the high points but in the endings, beginnings, detours, dead ends, and in-between times. His powerful tools are not just the promotions and graduations but the failures and firings and losses and sicknesses and shocks and periods of boredom. . . .

And during all His working—all God's silent activity in the disappointments, surprises, delights, irritations—transformations are taking place.

Anne Ortlund

MY FIRST NIGHT at home after being released was not exactly utopia for Lois and me. Our adrenaline was running too high to relax. All the excitement caused Lois to get sick with an upset stomach. She spent much of the night in the bathroom. I found myself getting out of bed frequently just to look through all the closets and under the sinks and cupboards. It was, I suppose, my way of getting used to calling this place home.

I did the same when I got outside, perusing all the new models of cars zooming in every direction. Eating ice cream in a coffee shop or just watching people coming out of stores were fresh, stimulating experiences. After three years of being cut off from the world, this seemed like a new planet. People who saw me must have thought I'd just gotten off the boat from somewhere far away. I noticed everything, including the cost of the do-it-yourself car wash, which in my absence had tripled from a quarter to seventy-five cents!

Those first few days I also looked over my shoulder more than a few times. In prison I'd waited for the doors of my cell to fly open and for someone to say they'd made a mistake. Now I was concerned that would happen in reverse. Spotting one of the prison guards shopping in a local K-Mart helped me get over that feeling.

Through our friends, God provided generously for our material needs. To our surprise, two days after my release, a minivan was delivered to our door, courtesy of Joe. It was gold-colored, like a crown. I was sure it would never need oil or run out of gas. After three years of constantly being searched, harassed, threatened, degraded, and dehumanized, driving this car was balm for my soul.

The First Baptist Church of Centralia, which had lovingly looked after Lois and the children, had been given the use of a small house, which it was holding for us. After the unfavorable verdict on October 3, they began looking for other alternatives. But some at the church believed in miracles and had kept the house available. On November 14 we moved in.

Dr. Royce Johnson, the ophthalmologist for whom Lois worked, and a Christian, hired me to assist with staffing the practice he owned with four other doctors. After three years of feeling useless in the scheme of things, I was energized by the knowledge that my efforts could make a positive difference in the lives of others.

Before I started, however, Lois and I enjoyed a two-week vacation at a Holiday Inn in Mt. Vernon, Illinois. We brought along our favorite baby-sitter so the children could stay in another room. It was like another honeymoon for Lois and me. But during that time we began to discover that both of us had become different people.

Most people can point to something in life they want more than anything else. Maybe it's the perfect job or the perfect house. Single people believe that meeting the right man or woman would solve all their problems. Infertile couples believe if they could only have a child, nothing else would matter. Life would be one big bundle of joy.

Usually, however, if and when we finally get what we want, the contentment is only temporary. We find that it takes more than one ingredient to produce happiness. The perfect job in time has a way of becoming mundane. The perfect house gets old in time. And even the best of children bring with them a whole host of problems and challenges the proud parents never dreamed of.

Nelson and Winnie Mandela's marriage lasted through twenty-six years of separation as they waited, seemingly without hope, for his freedom. Within two years of his release, the two were separated. Even multimillion dollar lottery winners typically end up discovering that no amount of money can buy happiness.

For three and a half years the only thing I wanted was to be free and reunited with my family. It would not matter what kind of house we lived in or how well we ate or if I could get a good job I enjoyed. Next to my freedom, these meant nothing. When I regained my freedom, I believed, life would be perfect always.

But eventually the afterglow of the first few weeks began to diminish. I could not spend the rest of my earthly days being happy about not being in prison. The realities of life would not allow that. With my freedom under my belt, other problems began to emerge.

Lois and I began to realize that our battle wounds would likely remain with us for a long time. Freedom would not be an automatic ticket to happiness.

Challenges presented themselves on several fronts, including from the children. They had been scarred by what they had been through, each in his or her own way. And we were not always sure how to assess the damage, much less how to repair it.

On Christmas morning, for example, Paul finally got his puppy. I brought Dutch up from the cellar at 4:30 A.M. after he'd barked all night long. He curled up on the couch with me. Paul awoke at 7, came downstairs, and plopped himself down on top of me. When he spotted Dutch for the first time, he was filled with delight.

But sometimes when he was holding Dutch, Paul would suddenly break into tears as big as raindrops. When I'd ask what was the matter, he'd say he was afraid that if we ever left this house, Dutch would be taken back to the dog pound, which Paul called the "doggy prison," and killed. I assured him that would not happen, but it took several such tearful episodes before he was convinced.

Vicki was just six months old when I was sent to prison. During the next several years, it seemed to me her life had been one big blur of being dragged along with Lois to meet with attorneys or keeping herself occupied on the floor while Lois talked on the phone. She perhaps sensed that her mother was preoccupied, emotionally distant.

Vicki was aloof and temperamental toward me. At times she appeared to resent me for intruding on her relationship with her mother. Though she called me Daddy, she was not really sure who I was. Her concept of a father was limited to someone you visit once a week. Even those visits had a distorting effect. Essentially all we could do was sit at a table. The environment was stilted. If the kids wanted something from the vending machine, they had to go get it themselves. Prison rules did not permit me to handle money.

For several months after I returned home, Vicki and I labored our way through this awkward relationship. Finally, about three days after one of the few spankings I've ever had to give her, I took her into my arms and began to explain to her what daddies are for. I spoke with her about other little girls whose fathers she knew, explaining that I was a father to her. I told her why I had been away while the other girls' fathers had stayed with them, like daddies are supposed to be.

As I continued telling her how much she meant to me, I sensed that she was understanding for the first time who I really was. I can still see her furrowed brow and her eyes darting around as she thought this new information over. Then she wrapped her arms around me and cradled herself tightly against my chest with her head buried in my neck. I held her and kissed her for several minutes, sensing the awesome significance of this moment for both of us.

The following morning, for the first time Vicki called for me to come to her when she woke up, and we repeated the hugging and kissing. Ever since then, she has always been the first to greet me when I walk through the door.

Paul and Vicki were younger and more resilient than our other child, Katherine, about whom I worried most. I had disappeared from her life when she was four, right at a time when it could cause the most emotional confusion. She was old enough to know that something terrible was happening, but not old enough to understand exactly what or why. I'd had some wonderful times alone with Katherine, as many parents do with the firstborn. Nothing delighted me more than to scoop her up into my arms and take her with me to the hardware store or the shopping mall. I remember embarrassing Lois once by playing hide-and-seek with Katherine in the clothing section of some department store. More so than the other children, Katherine knew me and missed me.

I remembered Katherine as having a simple, childlike faith. When she wanted something, she prayed for it and expected an answer. After I was imprisoned, Katherine developed a habit of picking a date—her birthday or Christmas—and convincing herself that by then I would be released. As several of those deadlines came and went, she stopped setting dates . . . And she stopped praying. The joyfulness of her childhood was tempered; her smile lost its energy.

I'd left behind an exuberant, joyful, carefree little girl and returned to a child who seemed distant and withdrawn, as if betrayed by something or someone. For the most part, she kept her hurt wrapped up inside. When she wrapped her arms around me, I sensed not just a hug of happiness, but a hug of pain.

Katherine's was a mature hurt, requiring longer sessions of talking, acceptance, and interaction. Lois and I observed that she had trouble expressing emotions. In obvious situations where we expected some expression of happiness or sorrow, there was nothing. Other times she would cry for no apparent reason. Katherine was one big reason I would return to school to pursue a degree in clinical psychology. I wanted to make up for the past as best I could; I wanted to understand and help my own family as much as possible.

Our problems were not limited to the children. Lois and I struggled as individuals and as a couple. With all the junk we had to deal with, we could have kept a family systems counselor busy for quite some time.

Marriage counseling ought to be a routine part of the post-prison experience. We were hesitant to seek this out, partly because we thought it displayed weakness, but largely because we feared the prosecution would find out about it and somehow use it against us at the next trial. So we attempted to go it alone.

In many ways Lois and I had to get to know each other all over again. We found that we could not simply pick up where we had left off. I was not the same man Lois had married. No one can spend the amount of time I spent behind bars without becoming a different person.

Being an ex-prisoner is in some ways comparable to being a Vietnam vet in that the effects can linger for quite a while. I had considerable emotional and attitudinal damage to repair.

My view of the world and of other people had been tainted in the crucible of a prison cell. I had learned that in order to survive, I could trust no one. To be suspicious, skeptical of others' motives, had by necessity become second nature to me.

Now I didn't have to think that way anymore. I was not surrounded by thugs and thieves. Instead, I was in the company of the people who loved me the most in this world. I knew that, and I wanted to live that way, as if nothing had happened, as if I'd never been away. But something *had* happened. I found myself still holding up the armor, instinctively putting emotional distance between myself, my wife, and my children.

In prison people learn not to care for others. No one can afford to get pulled into other people's problems. If the guy in the next cell cries all night or tries to hurt himself, that's his problem. In prison, I had only so much energy, and I needed it all to look out for myself. Now I found that when things were going crazy at the house or if there was conflict, my instinct was to look the other way.

I left prison an angrier man than when I'd entered. I'd been conditioned not to take anything from anyone. I never bothered people, but my feeling was that if someone tried to push me around, I'd teach him a lesson. When I walked out of prison, I carried those instincts with me. Lois noticed how quickly I judged people, how readily I questioned their motives, and how easily I resorted to anger.

Dealing with this anger rendered disciplining the children a confusing proposition. Sometimes I felt at a loss in determining the proper role of physical punishment. Lois and I have always believed that spanking has a legitimate role in parenting. But my view of its appropriate role was—pardon the pun—out of whack. One time after I gave Paul of couple of swats, I decided that I needed to step back for a while and let Lois continue to take leadership in this area. Discipline presumes the context of a secure, loving relationship. I wasn't sure I knew my kids well enough to spank them. And I feared they didn't know me well enough to understand a spanking.

Lois, too, had changed. She was not the same woman I had married. We'd visited almost every week, and even from prison I tried to keep close track of what was happening on the home front and to participate in important decisions when possible. I tried as often as I could to provide input into important family decisions. But now I realized how poor a substitute this was for being there.

The reality was that I had not been a part of my children's lives like Lois had been for over three years. I was not there to greet them in the morning or to tuck them in at night. I was not around to change dirty diapers, to handle the many minor crises that present themselves unannounced, or to experience the little pleasures parents ought to enjoy together. These seeds of marital and family growth had lain dormant in our lives for three and a half years. To get them growing again would not be easy.

In the early years of our marriage and parenthood, our family was, for the most part, patriarchal. That has a way of changing when the patriarch is behind bars. Lois had handled the transition with grace under pressure and with skill. She had developed her own systems for running the household. She knew what worked and what didn't work with the children. She knew how to balance the checkbook. She had established a track record of making the decisions that were best for the family.

Now it was unclear where this newcomer fit in. Lois viewed me in some ways as an intruder, a threat to the very family I had prayed so long to rejoin. She was, understandably, hesitant to relinquish control.

She certainly considered me a threat to the family finances. Prior to going to jail I was one of the most frugal people alive. But now I had what Lois called a "chemical urge to buy." With the freedom to make choices again, I was overcompensating, making up for lost time. I was insulted when Lois did not want my name to appear on our checks, but from her perspective she was, once more, looking out for the best interests of the family.

Some of our marital problems were related to Lois's expectations. Perhaps without realizing it, she expected me to emerge an ideal person with the wisdom and spiritual maturity of the Apostle Paul. She envisioned me taking my Bible each day and teaching the children the Scriptures. Instead, I spent most of my time in the morning watching television, out of habit, and wrestling with the kids. As far as Lois was concerned, mine was a mediocre spirituality at best.

This was magnified by the fact that I had also interrupted her morning quiet times, during which she had uniquely experienced God's closeness almost every day for a year immediately prior to my release.

Clearly, despite the many ways in which our spiritual lives had been enriched and our faith renewed as a result of my prison experience, there were side effects—major ones. They might be compared to the injury incurred by the surrounding muscles while a broken bone heals. When the cast is taken off, the biggest problem is solved, but in the process other problems rise to the surface.

Things came to a head one day when Lois stormed into the room, tore all her buttons off her blouse, and screamed, "I can't take it anymore." We chuckled as the buttons spun onto the floor. But then I took her into my arms, and she repeated her statement, in tears.

We were struggling as a couple and as a family. Our ordeal was not over; we still hurt. We were grieving even though no one had died. On the other hand, physical death might be viewed as a mere technicality. For truth be told, every day I'd been away, each of us had died a little.

In some ways death would have been easier for Lois and the children to understand and accept. People in general have more experience dealing with death, even in cases of premature death that seem unfair. Death, at least, has a physical explanation. We live in a largely cause-and-effect universe, dominated by physical laws that explain car accidents and medical diagnoses that explain deadly diseases. In contrast, the chain of events that led to my incarceration bordered on the absurd, defying easy explanation or belief.

Death, at least, is certain, definitive. It leaves no loose ends. Our ordeal—its cause and ultimate result—had been anything but certain. The emotional highs and lows, delayed court dates, and dashed hopes all pointed toward an almost fatalistic conclusion that nothing in life is certain.

Many books have been written to help Christians get through the untimely death of a loved one. Likewise, many have been written on how to begin a marriage. But there were none we knew of on how to resume a marriage after a three-and-a-half-year break during which the personalities of the bride and groom had been radically altered. We needed help, and we knew it.

Before going to a counselor, I decided to drive up to Chicago and talk things over with Joe, who seemed to have a special ability to see beneath the surface and isolate the heart of a problem. The following weekend, Joe flew down to meet with Lois and me. It turned out to be a watershed experience, especially for Lois.

Joe began by making sure that we were aware of all the implications of the adjustments we both were having to make. He encouraged us to understand that after what we had been through, we should not expect life to return to normal for a while yet. We needed to relax and be patient.

He spent most of the day, however, focusing on our concept of our identities in Christ. Lois's inborn intensity had served her well in many circumstances. But it worked against her with regard to the things she perceived God desired of her. Underneath that heavy armor of toughness, many of Lois's expectations about the way things should be—and the way I should be—were rooted in the view that, while God certainly loved her, that did not mean He liked her. Her primary concept of God was of a ruler and a judge, as opposed to a loving Father, her Poppa who cared about her far more than He cared about the things she might do or fail to do.

Lois was used to serving God out of a sense of obligation

instead of doing so freely, out of love. Years of trying to please Him melted away in tears of happiness and pain as Lois began to uncover the full implications of God's unconditional love for her. She felt brand-new.

In addition to this, Joe spoke with Lois with regard to her expectations of me. She freely admitted that she missed those times in the morning alone with God. And I freely admitted that there was no way I could replace those times, no matter how "spiritual" I might become.

Joe pointed out from Scripture that Jesus, while He found time to be alone, never rejected anyone who came into His life. Lois concluded that she was being somewhat selfish. After I come home, her times alone with God were never quite the same. She came to believe that He had come to her in her time of deepest need. But now that time was over, and it was time to return to me.

From that point on, Lois and I were able to relax. We set up regular times to meet with one another and to reflect on how we were feeling, what we were doing and why. This helped both of us to guard against the tendency to slip back into a view of God as a taskmaster instead of a loyal friend.

During this time we needed each other as much as ever, for though we had come a long way, we had a long way yet to go.

15

Desert Years

It's a hard road to travel but it must be done. It's the only
way to reach the other side.

Barbara Williams

FOR LOIS AND ME, working through the damage that had
been done to our marriage and family was complicated
by one haunting reality: the possibility that I would one
day have to return to prison. Despite the overpowering arguments in our favor, I knew all too well the foibles of the criminal justice system, with all its irregularity, instability, and
unpredictability.

Ultimately our arguments would be presented to and judged
by fallible men and women who might or might not be competent or corrupt. We knew we could take nothing for granted.

I received regular reminders that I was not out of the woods
yet. Each time I wanted to leave the state of Illinois, for example, I had to get permission from the Illinois Supreme Court.

Whether or not we should have, Lois and I felt the pressure
of our every move being watched by the state. In our situation
of legal limbo, we were fully aware that anything we said or did

could be used against us at the next trial. One result of this was that we were afraid to be seen or overheard arguing. This paralyzed the spontaneity of our relationship during a time when free communication was essential to our recovery.

In short, the uncertainty of our future accounted for a major source of stress in our lives. Not knowing if and when we might have to return to court, we could make no long-term housing or career plans. The realization that we might have to endure another period of separation caused each of us to hold back something in our relationship. We joked around a lot as a coping mechanism, a way of deflecting the stress, of avoiding the abysses of our past and our future. And when it came to avoidance, I was the ringleader.

For two years I worked at the ophthalmology office as we waited through delay after delay for the Illinois Supreme Court to make some kind of decision on the case. Vainly we speculated on possible reasons for the delay. Emotionally, I found myself becoming uncharacteristically tense and reactive.

I was also bothered by my inability to forgive my persecutors. Having made a conscious decision to forgive them helped greatly, but it took near-constant vigilance on my part to fend off feelings of unrighteous anger.

On October 17, 1986, our deepest fears were realized. Instead of upholding the decision of the appellate court, the Illinois Supreme Court ruled in favor of the state. In returning the case to the appellate court to decide whether it merited being tried again, the higher court reinstated the original, guilty verdict.

I was at work when I got the call. At first I was shocked. Then I began to feel sick with the realization that I would most likely have to return to prison.

I called Lois and asked her to get the children ready for a ride in the car. I wanted to drive to someplace scenic, so we could at least be in a beautiful place while I delivered this ugliest of news. My lawyers had filed requests that I be allowed to remain free until the appellate court issued another ruling. But we held out little hope of that happening, even as we wondered how God could allow the miracle of October '85 to be nullified.

We drove for an hour and a half to the Mississippi River and found a nice park. We laughed and played, skipped a few rocks, and watched some barges and boats go by. Finally, as Lois hung her head I sat the children down and explained as clearly as I could what had happened. For the next half hour or so, I answered their questions. Paul, now seven years old, squeaked out words I will never forget: "Dad, if you have to go back inside there, I'm going to be sick." With that, he held his stomach.

When we arrived home, I called Tom Decker and asked if there was anything we could do to improve our chances of bond being retained. Specifically I asked if letters to the court might help. Tom said this would not be a typical legal procedure, but that we should feel free to try anything under the circumstances. Feeling our pain, he was discouraged and not very hopeful.

In church that Sunday I announced that anyone who wished to write on my behalf should do so immediately. I was planning on going to Chicago the following evening for a hearing on Tuesday. By 4 P.M. Monday, over a hundred letters were ready to go. Additional letters were mailed as well. They came from my employers, from the former mayor of Centralia, from bankers, doctors, engineers, housewives, and retirees. Together they represented a cross section of the community in which I'd lived for five years, three of them as a prisoner.

Whether all those letters did any good, we may never know. But in a closed session the ruling came down in our favor. I could remain free on bond. God's miracle had held firm. We were happy and relieved, but it was hard to celebrate given that the high court's decision was ultimately a setback.

In 1987 I resigned from my job in order to complete my Bachelor's degree in psychology from Southern Illinois University in Carbondale before my benefits under the G.I. Bill were up. I had been going part-time, commuting from Centralia, about an hour away. We moved to the rural town of DeSoto, Illinois, so I could be closer to school. It was a good time to move, since our church in Centralia had just undergone a rancorous split, and we had friends on both sides.

Our time in DeSoto ended up being a relaxing and healing experience for our family as the Lord provided for us in many ways. The children enjoyed the rural living and the schools. Most of their teachers were believers who attended either the Southern Baptist church or the Christian Church in town.

We got involved with the independent Neighborhood Bible Fellowship in Carbondale. I did some circuit preaching for American Baptist churches in the area and eventually took an assignment as a pastor for a small American Baptist church for one year, mostly filling the pulpit and doing baptisms. In addition to attending school full-time, I worked as the advertising director at a small newspaper and also at a quick-mart near our home.

Despite the relative tranquillity in our lives, the case remained a constant preoccupation. A regular stream of letters flowed into our mailbox, overwhelming us. We tried to keep up with it, even though nothing new was happening.

One reminder of our case came in the form of a phone call from some guy who was, for all practical purposes, a bounty hunter. There had been a few killings in the area recently. This guy told me he had a financial interest in solving the case, and he said he had a theory. He went on to explain that he had been following our case, and he suggested that there seemed to be murders every place Lois lived. This crank's theory was that Lois was responsible for all these killings. He went on to say that he knew our schedules and had from time to time staked out our house.

Usually I was very guarded in how I expressed myself, for fear the prosecution would use it against me. But this guy made me so angry, I made an exception in his case. I told him three things. First, I suggested that, unfortunate as it is, murders probably occurred near the places he'd been living as well. Second, I suggested that if he thought Lois was a killer, he should take it to heart and stay away from our house. Third, I told him if he ever came around or if I ever saw him outside staking us out, I'd flatten his nose for him. I was determined not to have to add "being staked out by a crackpot" to our list of worries.

Media reports also kept the case alive for us and others. As time went on, the reports moved increasingly in our favor. ABC's "20/20" aired two segments on the case. Other television newsmagazine shows followed suit. The Chicago newspapers, as well as the downstate ones, accelerated their coverage of the case as well.

Finally, in July of '87, the Illinois Appellate Court came through with a positive ruling. It was very strongly worded, stating that the prosecution had "made up" evidence, that ideals of justice had been "trampled upon" at my trial. But, like the first time around, the decision was not unanimous. We hoped the state would simply drop the case, but their attorneys did not do so. Both sides knew that the Illinois Supreme Court had sided with the state previously. Now the issue, however, was not whether to uphold the original verdict, but whether to support the appellate court's decision to grant me a new trial. In any case, the Illinois Supreme Court was an unknown quantity.

Then came the emergence of new evidence: possible bite marks on the victim's body. This evidence came to light in 1987. Dr. Edmund Donoghue of the county's medical examiner's office, who seven years earlier had performed the autopsy on the body of Karen Phillips and testified at the trial, had maintained an interest in the case. He reexamined some old forensic photos, eventually determining that what had originally been listed as abrasions were actually bite marks. He offered this information to the state, which was obligated by law to offer it to us.

Magnuson, the chief prosecutor, made an offer to explore this course in an effort to "implicate or explicate" me once and for all. He probably thought we would run from this, but we immediately took him up on it. We were excited about the prospect of some hard evidence that could clear me.

We filed a motion before the Illinois Supreme Court to delay proceedings while we petitioned the appropriate lower court on the new evidence.

It took another year before we finally had our day in court. By then I had moved the family to Macomb, Illinois. Lois testified under oath that I had had no major dental work done since 1980. My dental records from the seventies confirmed that. Our experts testified that the bite marks on the victim clearly did not match my dental structure. They also testified, however, that the pattern of teeth was more indicative of a large animal than a person. Had they concluded that another human being was responsible, that unknown person would have likely replaced me in the eyes of the court as the prime suspect.

According to the state's experts, the bite marks were made by a human. But the state's attorneys would not allow their experts to compare the photographs with my dentition. On October 28, 1989, a judge decided against compelling the state to perform the test. This path having reached a dead end, we took our place in line again with the Illinois Supreme Court.

A few weeks later, on November 12, our fourth child was born. Rachel Alise was a joyful diversion from the tumult and frustration the case was causing. We prayed that she would be spared the turmoil her parents and siblings had to face.

As it had in the past, the waiting was taking its toll on me. I was frustrated. The legal hassles were preventing me from pursing a career and earning a decent income. I decided I could make the best of the situation by continuing my schooling.

That is why we moved to Macomb, so I could pursue a graduate degree in clinical psychology at Western Illinois University. Feeling robbed of life and choices, I was determined to achieve something tangible through the endless delays.

I came to regard the move to Macomb as a mistake. The children had grown weary of moving and had trouble making the adjustment to Macomb schools. After a year of taking classes, we moved yet again, this time to Springfield, where I started a one-year internship at the Springfield Mental Health Center in order to fulfill the requirements for my Master's degree.

I started the internship in August 1990. Oral arguments were held before the state high court in November. Based on past experience, we expected a decision in about seven months to a year. To our surprise, the court rendered its ruling just two months later, on January 31, 1991.

The good news was that the ruling was in our favor. The court agreed unanimously with what we'd been saying for almost ten years—namely, that I had been denied a fair trial, that statements made by the prosecution at my trial "so prejudiced defendant's rights that they alone are reversible and require remanding the cause for a new trial." The high court, in essence, ruled that the state's so-called "scientific evidence" was neither scientific nor evidence.

The bad news was that the state did not immediately drop the case as we'd hope it would do. Either they thought they could win based solely on the dream, or they just wanted to save face and deflect press scrutiny for as long as possible. Whatever the reason, it made it impossible for me to continue my internship.

This was a major disappointment. It was just one more example of how this case kept haunting us. We couldn't get out from under it. It affected our relationships with others, especially those we did not know well. We were forever unsure whether to talk openly about the case and were sometimes left to speculate on what others thought.

As the years wore on, living in limbo created more and more marital stress for Lois and me. The move to Macomb had been controversial for the family in the first place. We began to repress our feelings and emotions. Neither of us talked about it for a year. All we could do was hold on tight and hope the end would come soon. As the tension increased, we tried to concentrate on the most important matter at hand: the next trial. The state seemed determined to fight to the bitter end. Usually that fight took the form of delay after delay after delay. Trial dates began to be set for 1991.

Finally one was set for May 1992. My preparation had actually begun the previous December. For five months straight, I perused the transcripts of the previous trial, including the six hours of taped interviews with the police investigators. I was prepared to analyze each voice inflection and word pattern and to comment on psychological factors that might have influenced their questions or my responses those many years ago. I prepared myself more for this trial than for anything I've ever done.

Two weeks prior to the May trial date, the case took a new twist. The state had interviewed a forensic scientist from the original trial who said that a beaker used to store the vaginal smear might contain enough material to allow a newly developed DNA analysis to be performed.

This material probably could have been tested several years earlier, but opportunity fell through the cracks.

The state offered to let the DNA analysis determine the direction of the case. This process dragged on, as we had a very difficult time coming up with an expert who was agreeable to both sides and who was willing to do the tests. We rejected several of the labs suggested by the state because we felt they were too closely tied to law enforcement.

Each time a new trial date was set, we had to contact people across the country who were planning to fly in either as witnesses or observers. Finally, after this happened two or three times, the judge became incensed. He ordered the trial to begin, DNA tests or no DNA tests. But he relented and granted another delay when he sensed movement on the DNA front.

Finally state prosecutors and my attorneys agreed that a lab in Boston would perform the tests. In order to do so, scientists would first grow more DNA from the existing material. This would ensure that the substance was not consumed, a crucial factor in the event of a challenge to the test results.

For us to agree to the tests entailed some risk. There was no way the tests could establish conclusively that I was the semen donor. But, as it was explained to me, there was a 20 percent chance the test results could yield a false positive reading, failing to eliminate me. If this were to happen, it would almost certainly be used against me in court. On the positive side, there was roughly an 80 percent chance the tests would conclusively eliminate me as a possible semen donor.

Even though I had not been convicted of rape, the vaginal smear evidence was significant. It had played a central role in the state's claim to have scientific evidence against me. It is likely that the jury found me not guilty of rape based on their conclusion that the sex might have been consensual.

If the tests would establish that someone else had had sex with Karen Phillips, the state's case would be weakened even further, reduced to practically nothing aside from the dream. Nevertheless, based on their actions to this point, we never entertained for a moment the possibility that there would not be a second trial. We did not know if the DNA tests would be definitive. We did know they were very important to both sides.

The tests were finally done. As we awaited word on the results, we continued preparing for the trial. The court date had been set for the final time: July 22, 1992. Nearly twelve years after this horrible ordeal had begun, the end was in clear sight. Or so we hoped and believed.

16

Free at Last

I know that you can do all things; no plan of yours can be thwarted.

Job 42:2, NIV

AS WE GEARED UP for the impending trial, our lives, as well as the lives of our friends and attorneys, took on a fever pitch. Schedules were cleared, flights arranged, and witnesses coordinated. Hundreds of thousands of dollars in legal expenses and investigation fees, not to mention hundreds upon hundreds of hours of work by some of the best legal minds in the country, were about to come to fruition.

On Sunday evening, July 12, ten days before the trial was set to begin, Tom Decker called me from his office. "Steve," he said, "I called to let you know that I'm ready." Those words, coming from Tom Decker, instantly gave me a supreme, unfaltering sense of confidence. It was like seeing Sylvester Stallone in the movie *Rocky* run up the steps of the Philadelphia Museum of Art after those countless hours of roadwork, sit-ups, and jumping rope.

I knew that my attorneys had uncovered all possible facts,

thoroughly developed all possible lines of argument, and prepared for every possible contingency. There was absolutely nothing more that could be done. Otherwise, the words "I'm ready" would have never left Tom Decker's lips. He was ready to do what all defense lawyers dream about in law school: blow major holes through the case of the prosecution.

As it turned out, however, Tom was not done yet. The next morning he got a call from a former police officer who offered new, potentially incriminating information about the arresting officers in my case. This added even another dimension to our defense, and Tom pursued it with renewed intensity. Even on the day of the pre-trial hearing, Wednesday, July 15, he was getting additional information.

Meanwhile, Lois, the children, and I were getting ready to leave for the trip north to Chicago a few days early in order to go over any last-minute details with our attorneys. We had arranged to stay in some guest apartments usually reserved for missionaries. The car had been washed, the oil changed. We'd been to the bank to withdraw $300 for expenses.

I'd just loaded the last of the suitcases when one of the children called out from inside with a sense of urgency. I hurried in. Lois was on the phone, shaking with excitement. She handed the phone over to me. On the other end of the line was one of Tom's secretaries.

She said she would prefer that Tom tell me what she was about to tell me, but she and her colleagues were not sure what to do. Tom had called from the courtroom, she told me, informing them that the results of the DNA tests had come out in my favor. "Steve," she added, almost whispering, "the state has dropped the charges." She said that Tom was ecstatic, but they did not know when he would have been able to call me because he was still at the courtroom wrapping up some of the details.

The secretaries were concerned that before long we would get an avalanche of calls from the media. (They were right.) They wanted us to be prepared.

As I was talking on the phone, Lois was dancing around the room with the children, who were screaming as quietly as they could. Tom's secretaries were celebrating with tears of joy.

Immediately after hanging up the phone, it was my turn to dance with Lois around the room. After a few laps I felt compelled to make an intentional effort to allow this joyful news to sink in. I sat quietly for about fifteen minutes, basking in the feeling of this tremendous burden finally being lifted away.

Not long after we began celebrating again, I sighed and thought aloud, "I can't believe it's all over."

Lois appeared puzzled. I will never forget the look on her face. It was exactly the same look of bewilderment she had moments after the guilty verdict had been announced years earlier. "What did you just say?"

I repeated the remark, and then it dawned on me that Lois was hearing this news for the first time. All along she'd been celebrating because the DNA tests had come out favorably. The secretary had not told her the rest of the news. "Honey, the charges have been dropped," I said. "It's all over." As she processed this news, her momentary shock quickly transformed into ecstasy.

As things began to settle down, we gathered the children around in the living room, and we all got down on our hands and knees. I began to weep. For a moment, I sobbed uncontrollably.

The children seemed a bit scared. They'd never seen me express my emotions quite so intensely. I reached my arms around the entire family and said, "I'm sorry I got you guys into this, and I hope you'll forgive me." Then, huddled in that tight circle, we prayed together as a family, praising God and thanking Him for seeing us through to the end.

Soon Lois was crying along with me, and she assured me that this whole mess was not of my making. Although I knew that, I needed to hear her say it. I never imagined those many years ago that one phone call—an afterthought—could have produced the ugliness it did: the pain, the loss of income and career, and the separation from my family. All those years I'd lived with the nagging feeling that my stupid mistake was responsible, even if only a little bit. Though fully aware of the many ways in which we had grown closer to God through this ordeal, I wanted the people I loved most in the world to know I was sorry it had happened the way it did.

Back in Chicago, Tom was putting the finishing touches on our victory. After the state dropped the charges, he demanded a trial. By doing so, in accordance with Illinois law, I had to be tried for these charges within 120 days or never again. Had he not taken this action, the state could have resurrected the charges at any time. Despite assurances from the prosecution that this case was finished, Tom was taking no chances.

Several times over the course of the day, Tom, Joe, and I found excuses to talk with one another as we attempted to process what had happened. Although Tom was overjoyed on my behalf, I could not help but feel disappointed for him since he did not have his day in court. I felt a twinge of disappointment, too. It's the same way a football team would feel if it spent months preparing for the Super Bowl—physically, emotionally, and strategically—only to have the other team forfeit on game day. Against another attorney, the state might have tried it. Those who knew both Tom Decker and the facts of the case must have realized they didn't have a chance.

On the other hand, maybe they realized they didn't have a

chance period. The *Wednesday Journal,* an Oak Park newspaper that had covered the case thoroughly through the years, editorialized that the DNA evidence should not have been a factor in the state's decision to drop the case. What the DNA evidence did, according to the editorial, was to allow the state to "get off the hook politically," while avoiding what would have been a very embarrassing trial.

In announcing that the case was being dropped, Cook County state's attorney Jack O'Malley made the amazing statement, "We no longer have sufficient evidence to obtain a conviction." It should be abundantly clear to anyone that if the state did not have sufficient evidence in 1992, it *never* had sufficient evidence.

We hoped at least that all the information that had been gathered on other possible suspects could be put to good use. The state, however, so far has shown no interest in taking over our files in pursuit of the killer. Despite the pressure from the press, the police have so far declined to reopen the investigation. To do so would be to admit that for twelve years they were wrong. Pride would not allow that.

We have to date received no apology from anyone for the hurt this ordeal produced for our family. In fact, in remarks to the press after dropping the charges, prosecutors suggested that I was guilty after all and may have had an accomplice. As first demonstrated in the police interview room twelve years earlier, facts are irrelevant for those who have already reached a conclusion.

All afternoon long our phone rang off the hook as calls came in from virtually every imaginable news source. We recorded a general statement to the press, then screened our phone calls, picking up if we recognized the caller.

The Chicago affiliate of NBC set up a remote interview at

Springfield station WICS. On our way back we decided to pick up a quick bite at a local restaurant. We pulled into a place called Mountain Jacks, thinking we could get pancakes there. As soon as we set foot inside, we knew that this place was no run-of-the-mill pancake house.

The carpeting was thick, the decor plush. We knew we couldn't get out of this place for much less than $100. But we had the cash we had planned to spend on the trip. And we were dressed for the occasion, since we'd all put on our Sunday best for the NBC interview. So we decided this would be our celebration dinner and ordered steaks all around.

My only regret was that we had to rush through the meal in order to be on time for our Wednesday night prayer group. Those people at Cherry Hills Baptist Church had been praying for a complete dismissal for over a year. Now that our prayers had been answered in the way we hoped, we wanted to be in the company of our brothers and sisters and to rejoice with them.

A CBS television crew directed by a Christian man filmed us during our prayer meeting. Meanwhile, an ABC crew was camped out at the house all evening long. When the hour grew late, this crew finally came over to the church, but we had already left for home. When they called from the church to ask if they could come over, we decided against it, thinking that the kids had had more than enough excitement for one day. They talked me into returning to the church for a short interview. Despite my strong sense that their only purpose was to keep up with the competition, I obliged.

That was my last official act on what had been a very eventful day. We'd begun the day preparing for the long drive to Chicago, but we ended up staying at home. We'd danced and rejoiced and sung, and we'd also wept. We ate at the most expensive restaurant we'd ever patronized, we ran up our long-distance phone bill, and we appeared on all three major television networks. Now, at the end of one busy day and of twelve grueling years, at long last the time had come to rest.

17

Looking Back—
Seeing Him

You are not to strive to get love; we don't live that way. We live from a posture of knowing that we are loved. . . . You can accept yourself now as the new person you truly are in Him, just as the Father accepts you—perfectly.

Bill Gillham

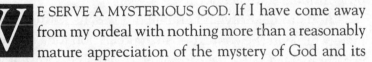E SERVE A MYSTERIOUS GOD. If I have come away from my ordeal with nothing more than a reasonably mature appreciation of the mystery of God and its implications, I would consider the experience indispensable to my spiritual maturity.

No one can fully comprehend the mystery of God. Even in acknowledging this fact we can do so with a certain smugness, as if in making the acknowledgment we have finally figured it out. Realizing that God is a God of mystery and experiencing that mystery, however, are two totally different things.

Our struggle lasted for twelve years. Its effects will remain with us for a lifetime. Some of those effects are positive, others negative. In any case, we will never be able to escape being defined by others—and defining ourselves—in terms of this experience.

To reflect on how we have been changed, on what we have learned, is both natural and inevitable. From the beginning we were open to what God had to show us and teach us. There was a time early in the heat of the battle when we half-expected one day to be able to pull out a piece of paper and make a list of all the things we had learned. These would be things that could be condensed into simple assertions, then recited one by one for the good of the church and others.

That would have been very nice and neat, but it is not the way God worked in our lives. Certainly we are not without a few summary affirmations of what we learned through our experience and what practical changes resulted from it. But the more significant changes in our lives have more to do with attitudes and outlooks on our faith, with fundamental adjustments in our understanding of our true identities as Christians. These changes can be discussed but cannot be easily reduced to direct, propositional statements.

Efforts to quantify and enumerate lessons learned are ultimately futile in the context of an appreciation for a mysterious, unfathomable God. One cannot go down a checklist attempting to find the "moral of the story" for each chapter of our suffering. I will attempt to offer some perspective on suffering in the closing chapter. But for now, suffice it to say that to some extent the purpose of our suffering remains a mystery, and the full answer to the question of whether it was necessary continues to evade us. We still hurt over it and to some extent wonder why it all had to happen as it did, even while firmly acknowledging that God's hand was working through it all.

But we wonder these things alongside our acknowledgment

of the good that has resulted. Though I cannot prove it, I fully believe that the Operation Greylord investigations into corruption in the Chicago Cook County court system were a result of prayer inspired by the case. As I and my family experienced the fruits of that system—fruits that often seemed rotten to the core—people all over the world prayed for peace in our lives and for justice. Among those convicted as a result of Operation Greylord was Judge Stillo.

Living through this ordeal changed my perspective on various sociopolitical issues, including the death penalty. We learned firsthand how easy it is for an innocent person to be convicted and put away for decades for a crime he did not commit. That I had an honorable discharge from the Navy and a clean record with respect to the law apparently counted for nothing.

I had friends, financial supporters, a strong family, and, once the first trial was over, the absolutely best lawyers available anywhere. I shudder to think of what would have happened to a black man who was equally innocent but who had no network of support and no access to funds required to ensure a competent defense. Had that been the case for me, I may have been dead by now, as I cannot imagine surviving the prison experience for three times as long as I did.

This is not to say that I oppose the death penalty absolutely. But many support it based on the notion that since this is America, the justice system must be fair and right. I have learned that it can be inequitable and arbitrary, if not corrupt, and unfair to many. What's more, plenty of those people who operate in the system are just as corrupt, though in different ways, as those they are trying to convict and have put to death.

We also came away with the realization that the system works against itself, in part by making "bad" people worse. "Rehabilitation" is a euphemism; "correctional institutes" do not correct a thing. I thank God for Prison Fellowship, Justice Fellowship, and similar organizations that are trying to shine Christ's light in the darkness. There may be more answers than we think. But we won't make significant progress until our society develops a collective will for change.

For both Lois and me, the most important lessons we learned through this ordeal are those related to our understanding of ourselves as children of a Heavenly Father who is all-loving and totally good. That part is no mystery, except to the extent that we cannot fathom the depth of His love and goodness.

Many evangelical Christians, even dedicated missionaries, approach Christian living as if they owe God forever and eternally. Motivated by guilt, they labor to please Him but are never quite able to find peace. Though they affirm that they are saved by grace, they behave as if their salvation depends on good works such as having a daily quiet time or faithfully attending church or a Bible study group.

The book *Birthright*, written by David Needham, recommended to Lois and me by Joe Ritchie, helped change our perspective in this area. I offer the following views humbly, recognizing that I am not a theologian and that some people I respect disagree with Needham at certain points. That said, his book helped us to understand fully the freedom we have in Christ.

Needham distinguishes between "positional truth" and "actual truth." Many Christians believe they are righteous only positionally—i.e., that God sees them as righteous through the lens of the Cross. Ultimately, however, in their day-by-day life, they find their identities in a sinful nature, a nature that God says has been crucified (Romans 6:6).

In contrast, Needham argues that biblically "[a] Christian, in terms of his deepest identity, is a SAINT, a born child of God, a divine masterpiece, a child of light, a citizen of heaven." He adds, "Becoming a Christian is not just getting something, no matter how wonderful that something may be. *It is becoming someone.*"

Based on this, I came to affirm that as believers we are not merely covered by Christ's righteousness. Rather, we are new creatures, with new identities in Christ. That is what it means to be born again. To put it another way, through Christ God created a new species—spiritual DNA and all—one that had not previously existed. Our primary identity in Christ is righteousness to the core. That is what a good God accomplished for his children through the Cross.

This is not to say we should never sing hymns like "Amazing Grace," for they remind us of the depths of God's love. Jesus Christ came to earth to save wretched sinners—each of us. And so we were. But that work is accomplished; it is done. He came so we would no longer have to call ourselves wretches.

To some, the difference between positional and actual righteousness may seem merely semantical. But both Lois and I came to recognize a genuine difference, one that revolutionized our concept of God and of how we should respond to Him. Instead of approaching Him out of obligation, we came to see that we could relate to Him out of love. Love is why a person should go to church, or read the Bible, or have a daily quiet time. The seeds of this truth were present in 1980, but we could not quite understand them. Our suffering helped put us in touch with who we are and were.

Sometimes I compare God to an earthly father who is wise, loving, and good and who loves all his children deeply. Each of his children is unique; each relates to him in a different way. Some are comfortable in his presence, whether they like to be near him and hold his hand or prefer to observe him, to laugh at his jokes, from the other end of the table.

Others, however, are obsessed with trying to please him. They constantly check themselves, wondering if they're doing it right. They scurry about, not realizing that all he wants is for them to relax, slow down, and join him at the table.

Had our twelve-year adventure not taken place, Lois and I would have probably ended up on the mission field working our tails off—doing some things wrong and some things right, but doing it all ultimately out of a sense of obligation and guilt. We would have been more concerned about the work, unable to see that what God desires most is for us to understand and enjoy our relationship with Him.

Our struggle to apply these revolutionary concepts to our lives helped Lois and me come to grips with another reality of Christian living. Through slipping back from time to time into our former patterns of guilty Christian living, we realized that the path toward Christ is not a straight, upward one. Rather, it's filled with surprises, winding around and up the mountainside with its many twists and turns and dips. We move ahead in fits and starts: three steps forward, two steps back.

Reaching one plateau does not guarantee that we will not someday have to reach it again. We must sometimes relearn lessons that have been forgotten. My striving to love the Giver, as opposed to the gift, represented a constant challenge in this regard.

As our path made its way up the mountain, sometimes it took us through places that brought pain and disillusionment. I learned that it was okay for me to ask the question "Why?" and to express my feelings freely in God's presence. Increasingly I realized that God understands our questions; more importantly, He cares. Beyond that, however, I learned that asking why is ultimately not necessary because God is gracious and good; He has only our very best in mind.

Many times I have wondered why God would allow so much time, money, and energy to be expended because of one almost whimsical phone call to the police. I have come to realize that we cannot judge God's purposes, nor where He places us, nor why He chooses one path for our lives as opposed to another.

The Bible itself is replete with accounts of divine action (or inaction) that does not seem fair, that does not make sense except when viewed in light of God's perfect plan. Thousands of Egyptian children were massacred while a baby named Moses was spared. Jacob was a liar and a thief, and yet it was he, not his faithful brother Esau, who received the blessing of their father Isaac and of God. On one level it makes no sense that God would allow His Son to die for the sins of humankind. But God has a plan—a perfect plan.

The weight of Scripture focuses not on how we can understand or control the things that happen to us, but on the kinds of people we should strive to be regardless of what happens. One thing Lois and I appreciated most about Joe Ritchie's counsel through this whole ordeal was that he never pitied us, never felt sorry for us or referred to what happened as a "tragedy." What happened had happened, and it was up to us to deal with it, to learn from it and grow from it.

Fundamental to such a perspective on the events of life is the affirmation that God is in control of the universe and of our lives. I believe that whether through His active or His permissive will, God controls every detail of my destiny.

Over the years many people have asked me what I make of the dream. Was it supernatural? Was it coincidence? Though I hesitate to answer with certainty, I personally believe that the dream was the result of demonic forces at work, attempting to cause permanent harm to my faith.

But though Satan is powerful, he is not omnipotent, and he can do only what God allows. This, no doubt, is what Martin Luther had in mind when he called him "God's devil."

I believe that God allowed enough similarities between the dream and the actual crime to lead a jury, in the hands of unscrupulous prosecutors, to convict me. He also demanded enough differences so that the truth would emerge like a light cutting through the darkness. And in the meantime He drew near to one of His seemingly insignificant servants and led him on an incredible journey—teaching him, weeping with him, rejoicing with him, and most of all loving him.

Lois and I believe that God revealed His faithfulness to us in many ways throughout this journey, including through some seemingly typical events of every day. While He did not keep us from suffering, He stayed with us in our suffering.

Our testimonies of how God reminded us of His presence appear throughout this book. One such reminder came after our ordeal ended.

In the summer of 1993, just after I'd started writing this book, I was walking past the Springfield Public Library and was drawn by its sidewalk sale of old books. I walked up to the table, and the first thing I noticed was the autobiography *Madame Guyon*. It is the story of a remarkable Catholic woman who more than two centuries ago was persecuted for nothing other than her devotion to Christ. Many consider the book a devotional classic.

Lois and I first discovered *Madame Guyon* in 1979. We took turns reading it in the car as we drove from Maine to Chicago on our way to Emmaus Bible College for the first time. We wept at her account of her sufferings. Madame Guyon also became a source of great strength to me during my time in Cook County Jail, where I read her book several times. Though separated by centuries, she became my sister and friend.

But it was not just the title of the book I recognized; it was this particular book—its creases and scratches. They say you can never tell a book by its cover. This one I could. I opened it up and, sure enough, there was the name "Steven Linscott" along with my prison number from Cook County Jail.

Over ten years earlier, I'd lent it to someone. It had made its way three and a half hours south to my backyard in much the same shape as I'd left it. This was like a visit from an old friend, replete with all the warmth and gladness experienced upon being reunited with someone with whom I'd shared so much suffering. I bought it back for fifty cents. (I still weep each time I read it.)

A coincidence? Perhaps. But for me it was yet another affirmation of God's faithfulness. And it was an occasion to reflect on everything my family and I had been through since I'd last seen that book. I realized that while I was a totally different person, God was ever constant, ever the same.

In late July of 1992, we had a final, joyful celebration service at which we received one of the most cherished gifts we've ever received. It wasn't money or clothes or jewelry. It was a gift of words.

A young woman, Mary Lynn Clever, who grew up in the church we'd attended in Oak Park those many years ago, has a unique gift for putting her reflections on Scripture into writing. She'd followed our story over the years, though we never met her until our final celebration, at which she read the following poetic reflection—based on Psalm 18—she'd composed only the day before:

Somewhere in the vastness of Your creativity, Your eye sees, and Your hand forms individuals—separate and unique—no two are exactly alike—and more unfathomable yet—You are intimate with each. In the larger picture of life You intertwine the lives of many, all the while keeping each separate and distinct in Your own mind, working for the goal of perfecting us, Your creation, for Your ultimate glory. In the intimacy that is Yours, You alone know the path—be it wide or narrow; be it steep or flat; be it rough or smooth—that each must tread.

Our confidence in the treading of our personal path is in You, our personal God. A God we know to be perfect. A God whose word is proven in our lives. A God worthy of our feeblest trust, when our eyes can no longer see the path. Others may look at our lives and question our footing, but faith can see where eyes are blind, and our confidence is in You, our God, our refuge and our shield.

At one point in each of our lives our path came to an abrupt halt. To take another step would mean to take an eternal plunge to sure destruction. You, our God, at that moment in time, spread out Your very life to bridge that gulf that we might continue our upward climb. How then at any point when our path seems impossible to traverse can we believe that, having once given Your very life for us, You would allow us now to stumble and fall?

It is a natural thing to look at the path You have chosen for another and condemn Your character. But only You—our Lord—know the purpose of that path and to what unforeseen glory it will lead. The surety of Your love secures his feet to his path.

Some may look at my path and become overwhelmed by the cliffs and cascades, but You have not equipped them to walk my path. You have fashioned my feet so that they will not slip, and raised me to the places I cannot climb. You have not created a path too steep for me, to see me fall, but a path just beyond my natural expertise that keeps me dependent on You, and in which I am needful of allowing the fullness of You to overtake that lacking in me. A simpler path would rob me of the intimacy with You that can only be enjoyed here on my path. Together—You and I—we climb the path; sometimes hand in hand, sometimes with me carried securely on Your strength. And be it wide or narrow, be it steep or flat, be it rough or smooth, we climb until together we stand at the top of the mountain called Life—ticking off but a moment of eternity—before stepping into the rest of infinity where we will share glory for time without end.

18

A Perspective on Suffering

> To be a man was something, to be a man of sorrows was far more; to bleed, and die, and suffer, these were much for Him who was the Son of God; but to suffer such unparalleled agony—to endure a death of shame and desertion by His Father, this is a depth of condescending love which the most inspired mind must utterly fail to fathom.
>
> Charles Spurgeon

IN THE APRIL 26, 1993 issue of *Christianity Today* magazine Marshall Shelley told the story of his third child, a daughter named Mandy, who was simultaneously the source of much pain and much growth in the lives of her parents and their friends.

Mandy was born with microcephaly (a small head). She was severely retarded. The Shelleys learned early on that she would never walk or talk, nor even sit up or use her hands. In addition, Mandy experienced regular seizures, some of which required emergency trips to the hospital. She had cataracts removed from her eyes at three months of age, though her parents never knew if she could see or hear.

195

When Mandy was a year and a half old, she lost the ability to swallow, requiring that her mom and dad learn to feed her and administer medications through a tube in her nose. This tiny child, not surprisingly, brought many tears into her parents' lives, and also many questions.

But through their faith in God, the Shelleys were able to find some answers or at least to find contentment when surrounded by questions that remained unanswered. The article details the amazing number of people whose lives were changed and turned toward Christ because of this child's ministry. Mandy's father wrote that she "had an amazing ability to turn people's thoughts to God and to instill lasting lessons about our Heavenly Father."

People whose lives had been broken, who had abandoned God or felt abandoned by Him, one after another sought Him again because of the questions and issues this child raised in their lives. Among these people were health care professionals who were with Mandy during her final hours of life. Reflecting on that time the author writes, "In the presence of a dying child, a child who couldn't speak, we had a small 'revival'—people confessing sins and drawing nearer to God."

Even after Mandy's death, reports continued to come in about the positive influence she'd had on the lives of others. The author concludes the article by stating that "the greatest teacher of theology I know lived in our home. She stayed for less than two years, but her influence is eternal."

Such stories reveal a sort of paradoxical relationship Christians have with suffering and heartache. No one would ever hope to have a child like Mandy. No parents are joyful upon discovering their newborn baby has Down's syndrome or some other physical or mental handicap. The standard reply to the question, "Do you want a boy or a girl?" is, "We don't care, as long as he or she is healthy."

And yet, once blessed by the presence of a child who is not "normal," virtually all parents, including the Shelleys, will testify that they would not trade their experience for anything. The realizations, feelings, and reflections spawned by a vulnerable child, God's most productive theologian, are unique and perhaps could have come to us in no other way.

Theologian Jürgen Moltmann, reflecting on the various gifts God has given to his people, refers to "the gift of disabled life." He contends that people who are challenged with mental or physical disabilities enable all of us to discover God in ways unknown to us prior to our encounters with such persons.

Similarly, in the counseling I have done, I have found that those Christians who live with emotional and spiritual pain—perhaps because they struggle with some form of addictive behavior—when they are at last in control of their lives tend to be more spiritually in tune with God. They have had to tear away all the façades in an effort to gain access to God's love and power. They are living in the real world with real problems, problems that cut to the very core of their beings. They do not have time and energy to waste spouting truisms or echoing the pat answers that pour forth from those who do not know what it means to struggle.

When the state dropped its case against me, the cloud I had hanging over my head disappeared. Everything we'd invested into preparing for another trial—the time, the effort, and the research—was suddenly irrelevant. I could once and for all put behind me any prospect of having to spend more time away from my family because of this case. I could step over into Missouri or Iowa or Wisconsin or Indiana if I wanted to without having to ask anyone's permission. I was, after almost twelve years of struggle, finally free. This thorn in my side that most times had felt like a spear in my heart was finally gone.

And I would miss that struggle. For though it had been an enemy, it had also been in some strange way a friend. It had forced me, day after day and year after grueling year, to keep my eyes urgently focused on Christ and on the Father's desires for my life. Though it had been a source of confusion and intense emotional suffering, it had also been a catalyst for self-understanding and for personal and spiritual growth, growth that perhaps could have come no other way.

As I celebrated my legal freedom with my family and friends, I did so fully realizing that I had possessed the most important kind of freedom all along. DNA tests or no DNA tests, true freedom had been and would always be mine in Christ; in Him I had and will always find maximum security, which is not an imprisonment but liberation and life! In contrast, many in this world who have never and will never set foot inside a jail live within prisons of their own design.

There are prisoners of materialism who, because of an obsession to want more, are not free to enjoy the Giver. There are people imprisoned by selfishness and greed who will never be free to experience the joy that comes from sacrificial giving to the truly needy out of love for the greatest Giver. There are prisoners of mediocrity who are satisfied with something less than what God wants them to have in terms of their relationship with Him.

Others are prisoners of their own success, people who have never had occasion to peel away the layers surrounding their souls. They may never feel the joy that comes from the discovery of previously hidden truths about themselves or about their Creator. Walls of freedom can shield us from what is ultimately most important. And those walls can be as impenetrable as any prison wall.

I hope my words here do not make it seem as if I think I have already arrived at the place where God wants me to be, for certainly I know I haven't. My life has been changed forever; I will never be what I used to be. But I'm still on a journey, and I still have a long way to go. Perhaps other tragedies await me in the near or distant future through which God will draw me even closer.

This is not to imply that growth comes only through suffering, nor that suffering necessarily produces growth. To assert any precise cause-and-effect relationship between the two, I believe, is to fall into the trap of trying to put God in a box, to contain His ways, to make Him predictable according to our formulas and expectations. It cannot be done.

And yet, though we see through a glass darkly, we still see something. And perhaps some of what we see—distorted though it is—has meaning for our lives, particularly if we are content to examine it with humble eyes.

Most theologians ultimately regard the reality of suffering and evil in the world as a mystery, a "problem." But they also believe, as I do, that we can make a few Scripturally-based affirmations about the role suffering can play in the development of faith without being guilty of trying to control God. To the extent that we can understand even in small measure why God might allow suffering in our lives, we increase our capacity to accept that suffering and our openness to grow as a result of it.

We may also come to an appreciation of how God may be working in the lives of others who are suffering. Such appreciation might result in a healthier view of how to respond to those persons. If God is at work in their suffering, perhaps we should reevaluate the goal, rooted in instinct, of trying, above all else, to relieve that suffering.

I am reminded of the illustration (from *Knight's Book of Illustrations*) of the Emperor Moth. Before taking to the air, this beautiful creature struggles immensely to escape its cocoon. For days it tries to break out, and with each failed attempt a life-giving, strengthening substance finds its way to the moth's wings.

One day someone noticed the frantic struggling of one particular moth, felt pity, and decided to ease the moth's burden by cutting two slits on each end of the cocoon. The moth got out quicker, but its wings never developed. Instead of soaring through the air with rainbow-colored wings, it lived a miserable, bloated existence.

Perhaps what people who are suffering need most is not relief but encouragement. And they need others to accompany them in their struggle to the extent that is possible. Joe, for example, never felt sorry for Lois and me. What would that accomplish? He knew that as we were able to accept what had happened, we would give ourselves a chance to grow from it.

As for the above-mentioned Scriptural affirmations regarding suffering, it must be stated that one of God's purposes for allowing suffering is to deal out punishment. Suffering was a consequence of the first sin in the Garden of Eden. And the nation of Israel in the Old Testament made a virtual habit of suffering the wrath of God for its disobedience.

Unfortunately, some Christians jump quickly to the conclusion that suffering is always the result of sin, as if punishment is the only possible explanation for suffering. The Bible hardly supports this view. For one thing, the One who suffered most in the history of the world was sinless.

Another Biblical role played by suffering is that of discipline. Though they are similar concepts, the Scriptures clearly distinguish between punishment and discipline. Punishment has only negative connotations. It implies action from God toward people whose hearts are hard, who have turned their faces away from their Maker.

Discipline, in contrast, can consist of positive reinforcement as well as punishment. It implies actions rooted in love and intended to develop those who are moving toward maturity. The targets of discipline have not necessarily turned completely away from God. But they need occasional help to stay on the right path. Perhaps the best Scriptural support for this view is found in Hebrews 12:5, 6: "My son, do not regard lightly the discipline of the Lord, and do not lose courage when you are punished by him. For the Lord disciplines him whom he loves, and chastises every son whom he receives" (RSV).

In his book *The Way of Christian Living*, John H. Timmerman views discipline through the metaphor of Jesus as the Vine and His followers as the branches. "The life of the Christian needs pruning," writes Timmerman, "in order to bear abundant fruit." He continues:

> Sorrow is the hard pruning; none of us escapes it. It comes in different forms to different people. For some it is death, for others it is terrible loneliness, for others the bleakness of unrelieved depression. None of us escapes the seas of sorrow that engulf our lives. But the prophet Nahum tells us that God's "way is in the whirlwind and storm. . . . He rebukes the sea and makes it dry" (Nah.1:3-4). And Zechariah tells us that "his dominion shall be from sea to sea" (Zech. 9:10). During the times when sorrow seems to drown us, when bad things happen to good people, when the pruning shears seem to nip too close to the heart, the Christian can proclaim that God's way is in the sea, that God reigns, and that God will never forsake us.

While punishment and discipline explain suffering in essentially negative terms, the Bible also supports a more positive view of suffering. There is no greater symbol of suffering than the Cross. And as Christians, we are called to take up our own crosses and follow Christ.

Suffering provides us with a point of identification with the road our Savior traveled. "By suffering," writes van de Beek, "especially suffering in secret, people mature—they learn to accept; they live, not in mindless resignation from which all hope has been drained, but in a hope that bears all things. . . . In the experience of suffering, what finally remains is the relationship with Jesus Christ, who chose the road of suffering, but knew the joy which lay before him (Heb. 12:2) and so persevered. . . . We need not run from the suffering of the world; we can actually take it to heart. And the more the suffering of the world penetrates our hearts, the more we experience that through this suffering God will let us be his children. . . . The more we take upon ourselves the burden of this world's suffering, the more we mature in leaning on him who is the Lord of the world."

Van de Beek continues with this amazing statement: "Thinking about suffering in this way, we might get the idea that we should be delighted with the suffering we experience. In the final analysis, this conclusion is correct." As the Apostle James put it, "Count it all joy."

Yet it would seem that we are not called to seek suffering. Christ asked the Father to "let this cup pass" from Him. Someone who seeks martyrdom ends up not as a martyr but as a suicide victim. But when suffering comes our way, we are free to view it joyfully.

We may choose, based on our faith, to view suffering as an opportunity to grow closer to God. We may choose to take risks on God's behalf that might expose us to suffering, whether physical or emotional. After all, true heroism ought not be defined in terms of enduring hardship, but in terms of being willing to suffer sacrificially for the sake of others. That being the case, the Creator of the universe who came to earth to die for our sins is the ultimate Hero. God's willingness to become fully human and to suffer—undeservedly—intense physical, spiritual, and emotional pain is the starting-point of our faith.

Despite my appreciation for the good that can result from suffering, however, I cannot honestly say that all of my suffering throughout this ordeal made sense. So many times our hopes were raised, only to be dashed. It seemed so unnecessary and so unfair. Why, for example, would God allow a corrupt judge to sentence me to forty years? Why not have a decent, honorable man do the deed? That might have been easier to take.

Life, however, is not fair by our standards. We think that bad things should happen only to bad people and good things to those who are moral and upstanding. Yet what if things really worked that way? As Yancey puts it in *Disappointment with God*: "Imagine a world designed so that we experience a mild jolt of pain with every sin and a tickle of pleasure with every act of virtue. Imagine a world in which every errant doctrine attracts a lightning bolt, while every repetition of the Apostles' Creed stimulates our brains to produce an endorphin of pleasure."

In a world such as this—with a God created in the image of B. F. Skinner—there would be no need for the Moral Majority. But we must also ask if in such a world there would be any space left for human beings to love. That which is achieved by force cannot be love. Genuine love is freely chosen. God wants us to obey Him not so that we will be spared an electric shock, but because of who He is and what He has done.

Though some of the specifics of my suffering did not make

sense, prompting me to ask, "Why?," underlying it all was my firm conviction that God was calling me to come closer. Early on He got my attention. It was as if He were saying, "Watch what I can do. I will show you My power, and you will experience My love and faithfulness."

Furthermore, we must never forget that God's love for us is demonstrated by His willingness to suffer alongside us. Despite the theological "problem" of suffering, scholars agree that our God is a suffering God, a Father who hurts when we hurt, including in times of discipline. When I almost went crazy in Cook County Jail, God understood. When I was lonely or feared for my life, I believe God was lonely and afraid with me. Such belief is totally consistent with the character traits of the God described in Scripture.

We, on the other hand, tend to expect God to feel our pain without our feeling any sense of obligation to identify with His pain. God must feel hurt by a human race that has largely rejected Him, that is destroying His creation, and that is worshiping other gods while ignoring His commandments. We need to draw closer to God's pain, for shared pain brings relationship. It helps us to discover that we—God and us—exist and work together.

As I draw this book to a close, I do so acknowledging that these meager reflections will doubtless accomplish little in the way of satisfying scholarly theologians' quest for a solution to the problem of suffering. But for now, they are answers enough for me, and maybe they will serve to enlighten or encourage others.

In sum, perhaps part of God's purpose was to discipline me, to expose arrogant and judgmental attitudes that were affecting my ability to serve Him well. Perhaps He also wanted to use my suffering to draw me toward a greater appreciation of *His* suffering. And perhaps some aspects of my suffering, of wondering why certain things had to happen as they did, will, for now, have to remain mysteries.

I know only that I have a greater appreciation of His love for me and of my true identity as a believer than I ever could have had without this experience. And I have arrived at this point in my faith largely as a result of suffering.

Prisons, after all, are not meant to be pleasant places, and indeed they are not. Even a "country club" prison is still a prison. People may criticize these institutions, but you won't see them maneuvering to get into one.

I have spent half of my adult life fighting for my freedom as a result of being convicted for a crime I did not commit. Three and a half years—years that many would regard as the most important and productive with respect to family and career— were effectively washed away. I think it is fair to say that few people appreciate their physical freedom more than I.

But my concluding testimony is that the freedom for which I fought so hard and so long is nothing compared to the life-changing power of the freedom and security found in Jesus Christ.

Urban ministry specialist Ray Bakke tells the story of soldiers who spent the last part of World War II in a German prison camp. Unknown to the guards, these men had access to news from the outside through a wireless radio. One day the news came over the radio that the war had ended. The prisoners knew they would soon be free, even though the guards did not know it yet.

Bakke states that "the prisoners' behavior changed dramatically. They walked around the prison camp singing and shouting, they waved at guards, laughed at dogs, and did not complain about the food. Good news had given them hope, and hope changed them."

Good news—in fact, the very best news—is ours in Christ. At times in my prison experience that news gave rise to joy more exuberant than can be contained by any prison walls. Because of that, no one need feel sorry for me. I certainly do not feel sorry for myself. Instead, my heart goes out to those who have not discovered this freedom, the security of the power and love found in Jesus Christ. Without that, nothing else matters.

I close with a final memory of my time at Centralia. It was a weekday afternoon, and Lois and the children were getting ready to go home after their weekly, four-hour visit. Paul was almost five years old at the time.

He looked forward to these visits intensely, even though there wasn't a lot for a little kid to do. They weren't allowed to bring in toys. Sometimes an orange or an apple from the vending machine would have to suffice for a ball. And yet he never wanted to leave.

This particular day, he clung to my leg like his life depended on it, crying hard because he didn't want to go. I told him he had no choice, but that didn't register with the little guy. Finally, out of options, I looked down at him and said, "Paul, if you don't let go, I'm going to have to spank you."

He looked up at me with tears streaming down his cheeks—fighting for breath as crying children do—and forced out the question, "If you spank me, can I stay?"

He'd counted the cost, he knew the risks, and still he wanted to be with his father. May God grant each of His children the courage and the grace to do the same.

A CHRONOLOGY
OF EVENTS

July 9, 1954	Steve Linscott is born in Newport, Rhode Island.
July 30, 1974	Steve enlists in the Navy after two years of college.
November 24, 1974	Steve becomes a Christian.
1974–1976	Steve spends a two-year tour of duty in Japan.
February 23, 1977	Steve marries Lois Beverly.
March 1977–March 1979	The newlyweds live in Guam, where Steve is stationed at a U.S. naval base.
June 12, 1978	The couple's first child, Katherine Renee, is born.
March 30, 1979	Steve receives an honorable discharge from the Navy after five years of service.
August 1979	Steve enrolls at Emmaus Bible College in Oak Park, Illinois.

December 30, 1979	Paul Mark Linscott is born.
October 4, 1980	Karen Ann Phillips is murdered.
November 24, 1980	Steve is arrested and sent to Cook County Jail.
January 9, 1981	Steve is released from Cook County Jail after $45,000 bond is posted.
April 8, 1981	Steve takes a polygraph test, the result of which strongly indicates he is telling the truth.
January 28, 1982	Victoria Christine Linscott is born.
May 24, 1982	Steve goes on trial for three counts of murder and one count of rape.
June 16, 1982	A jury convicts Steve of murder; he returns to Cook County Jail.
November 23, 1982	A judge sentences Steve to forty years in prison.
December 6, 1982	Steve is transferred to Joliet Correctional Center.
December 20, 1982	Steve is transferred to Centralia Correctional Institute.
March 1, 1985	The case is heard by the Illinois Prisoner Review Board.
August 7, 1985	Illinois Appellate Court, in a 2-1 decision, overturns the guilty verdict. Steve remains in prison while the state appeals the case.

October 31, 1985	Bond is granted while the case in on appeal.
November 1, 1985	Steve returns home after nearly three and a half years of incarceration, but is not permitted to leave Illinois without permission.
October 17, 1986	Illinois Supreme Court reinstates guilty verdict, but returns the case to the appellate court to consider whether Steve should get a new trial.
November 12, 1986	Illinois Supreme Court denies the state's motion to revoke bond; Steve is allowed to remain free.
June 1987	Steve enrolls at Southern Illinois University to complete undergraduate degree in psychology.
July 29, 1987	Illinois Appellate Court concludes that American ideals of justice had been "trampled upon" and grants a new trial. The state appeals to the Illinois Supreme Court.
May 1988	Steve receives his B.A. in Psychology.
August 1989	Steve enrolls in graduate study at Western Illinois University.

October 27, 1989	Evidence regarding bite marks on the victim is nullified. The doctor who performed the autopsy on the body of Karen Phillips had previously regarded these bite marks as abrasions. Experts agreed they did not match Steve's dentition, but could not agree if they were made by a human being.
November 12, 1989	Rachel Alise Linscott is born.
January 31, 1991	Illinois Supreme Court upholds appellate court decision to grant a new trial. After numerous delays a trial date is finally set for May 1992.
May 1992	The state produces material from original trial and proposes DNA tests. The trial is delayed again, with the final trial date eventually set for July 22.
July 15, 1992	DNA tests fail to implicate Steve as a suspect. One week before the scheduled trial, the state drops all charges, ending the Linscott family's nearly twelve-year ordeal.

POSTSCRIPT

NE OF THE QUESTIONS I am asked most frequently is, "Have you ever considered pressing charges against the state of Illinois for false imprisonment?" The answer is, "Not for very long." In Illinois, the maximum award granted to victims of false imprisonment is a scant $3,000 for every year of incarceration. That amount would barely even begin to cover the attorneys' fees required to win the case.

Long-time Illinois governor Jim Thompson, who came up through the ranks of the attorney general's office, during his time as governor saw through legislation that allows police investigators and state prosecutors great liberties with limited fears of legal risks. This was possible in part due to public sentiment that the biggest problem with the justice system is with guilty people walking free rather than innocent ones going to jail. In my opinion, Illinois has gone too far. If there is another state that gives such free reign to prosecutors, I don't know what it is.

Over the years, my frustrations with the criminal justice system have, not surprisingly, given rise to more than a few ideas about how to change that system for the better. These ideas are not intended to make things easier for defendants or for prosecuting attorneys. Rather, they are meant to make the system more fair, in part by increasing its efficiency.

The following proposals represent some of my ideas in this regard:

1. Establish professional jurors or panels of judges.

Jury selection these days has become increasingly problematic. Virtually anyone who knows or believes anything about anything is perceived as being incapable of making a fair decision. Thus many of the most competent people are typically denied the opportunity to serve, increasing the "ignorance quotient" among jurors, although the trend in Illinois is toward limiting exclusions, including for doctors, lawyers, even judges.

In any case, getting out of jury duty has become a veritable art form, and the bottom line is that many juries do not represent a fair cross section of peers. Instead, they represent the bottom of the barrel.

Professional panels would ensure a certain level of competence among people who are determining the fates of others. Those who are trained for such work would be less prone to falling prey to attorneys' sophistry, and more likely to base their decisions on the laws of the land, the rules governing fair trials, and, most importantly, the facts.

When functioning at their best, they would recognize areas in which they are not qualified to reach conclusions—e.g., in instances of highly technical, specialized, scientific evidence. In such cases, they would be more likely either to request clarification or base their decisions on other factors. I realize that these panels might not be any more "professional" in their abilities than current jurors, short of guaranteeing them competitive wages.

2. Create judicial oversight committees for the purpose of restoring fundamental fairness and common sense to the courtroom and the legal process.

The justice system is driven by technicalities, some of which militate against discovering the truth and ensuring that justice is done swiftly. Perhaps the best known example is the guy who is clearly guilty, but because someone did not read him his rights in the proper fashion he is released. There are many, many more examples.

Rules and regulations are wonderful servants; they are very poor masters. Judicial oversight committees would be invested with the authority to determine if the rules are being used to serve the cause of justice or to serve the cause of some attorney.

Various rules, for example, dictate both the speed and the procedures according to which an appeal could be filed. A judicial oversight committee could determine when the appeals process should be hastened.

In my case, major new evidence was introduced shortly after the trial, evidence establishing that the state's scientific evidence was meaningless. In light of such new evidence, I should not have had to wait so long to get the case reconsidered. One function of the judicial oversight committee would be to see to it that cases wherein there have been significant new developments are granted priority in the appeals process.

In some ways, the role I am proposing for these committees is similar to that of a trial judge. But increasing the number of trained people responsible for overseeing cases is an insurance policy against an incompetent or corrupt judge.

3. Take steps to ensure a speedy trial.

Justice delayed is not justice. Attorneys, whether prosecuting or defense, routinely use stalling tactics for strategic purposes. State's attorneys are fond of citing their workloads as being the reason for their delays. Everything possible should be done to eliminate these excuses. Perhaps the only answer is to hire more attorneys for the state.

In any case, once that is done—or even if it cannot be done—judicial oversight committees could be charged with determining whether delays are sought for legitimate reasons or if they are mere stalling tactics. Of course, these committees could then take appropriate action to force the hand of whoever is stalling.

4. Establish a merit system for judges.

It is widely known that judges rise up through the ranks not because of their competence, but because of political consider-ations. No one should have to be persuaded that this is wrong.

Judges might, in one sense, be compared to baseball umpires. They are not supposed to favor one side or the other, but are assigned the task of making sure the game is played fairly.

On occasion, major league baseball players rate the umpires. Each player is asked to rate these umpires, some whose calls they liked and some whose decisions they didn't like. But the issue is competence.

Similarly, blind surveys of both defense and prosecuting attorneys could reveal which judges have the respect of both sides. Such a system is more likely to weed out corrupt judges and send incompetent ones back to traffic court where they belong. It would be a far better system than politics for deter-mining judges' career paths.

5. Encourage efforts to discover the truth, instead of to win cases.

There is a story, perhaps apocryphal, about Abraham Lincoln in his early years as a lawyer. Back in those days, the story goes, there was no concept of attorneys who worked strictly for the defense or the prosecution. A lawyer simply represented a person, regardless of which side of the law that person was on.

One morning Lincoln argued a case for a client masterfully, and the judge accordingly decided in his favor. That afternoon, however, a case exactly like the one Lincoln had argued in the morning came up before the same judge. Only this time Lincoln's client was on the other side. Lincoln stood up before the judge that afternoon, and the first words he said were, "Your honor, this morning I was dead wrong."

Whether or not this story is true, it illustrates the adversarial nature of our justice system. The primary goal of most attorneys is not to discover the truth but to win a case. And that is wrong.

Prosecuting attorneys should pursue the truth with the interests of the state in mind. Defense attorneys should pursue the truth with the interests of their clients in mind. But neither side should suppress the truth or manipulate facts in an effort to create a particular version of truth, which in fact is not truth at all.

Ultimately, I suppose, these are matters of the heart, of personal integrity and honesty. But certain actions could be taken to minimize the effects of a system in which both sides regard the truth as secondary to winning.

For one thing, attorneys who knowingly disregard or manipulate the truth—or even if they do so out of incompetence or willful neglect—should be subject to far more severe penalties.

In addition, I favor a move in the direction of a British system of law, in which one lawyer, the "solicitor," prepares the case and another, the barrister, argues it. With such a system, no one individual would have so much of his ego invested in the case to be tempted to win at all costs.

Some of my proposals, I realize, could cost a lot of money.

But they might save a lot of money, too, by eliminating unnecessary court procedures and lengthy appeals, and by increasing the efficiency of the system. After all, had the system worked for me, the state could have saved a lot of money in room and board for three and a half years. I would have been paying taxes instead of using tax dollars. Regardless of whether certain plans would save money, it is hard to put a price tag on fairness.

By and large, Christians have not given the issue of reforming our justice system the priority it seserves. Organizations such as Prison Fellowship and Justice Fellowship need our support. We need to pray for our justice system and condsider how we might work to improve it according to scriptural principles.

My proposals are by no means exhaustive. And many would argue that they are unrealistic for various reasons. But perhaps they could serve as food for thought, as a jumping off point for those who care enough to help the justice system live up to its name.